Dodgers®

FROM COAST TO COAST

Right-hander Greg Maddux pitched in the shadows at Dodger Stadium on August 13, 2006.

Mike Piazza hit two home runs and the Dodgers celebrated a 12-1 victory over the Giants on the final day of the 1993 season, which knocked San Francisco out of the playoffs.

Orlando Hudson pointed to the sky after he slid in safely at third base to complete the cycle (single, double, triple and home run) against the San Francisco Giants on Opening Day 2009 at Dodger Stadium.

Don Mattingly greeted his players on Opening Day 2011, his first regular-season game as the manager of the Dodgers.

Ebbets Field, 1938

Dodgers

FROM COAST TO COAST

THE OFFICIAL VISUAL HISTORY OF THE DODGERS

FOREWORD BY **TOMMY LASORDA** · INTRODUCTION BY **VIN SCULLY**

SKYBOX PRESS, SAN DIEGO · ABRAMS, NEW YORK

Library of Congress Cataloging-in-Publication Data available.

Memorabilia images courtesy of the Gary Cypres Collection. Used with permission.

ISBN: 978-1-4197-0322-5

Manufactured in China

10 9 8 7 6 5 4 3 2 1

Published by Skybox Press, an imprint of Luxury Custom Publishing.
Distributed in North America by Abrams, an imprint of ABRAMS.

3920 Conde Street
San Diego, CA 92110
www.skyboxpress.com

ABRAMS
THE ART OF BOOKS SINCE 1949
115 West 18th Street
New York, NY 10011
www.abramsbooks.com

TABLE OF CONTENTS

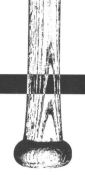

Hall of Famer Tommy Lasorda made his entrance onto the field during 50th anniversary introductions on Opening Day 2008 at Dodger Stadium.

FOREWORD
BY **Tommy Lasorda**

I first heard about the Dodgers when I was a kid growing up in Norristown, Pennsylvania. I knew practically every guy's name in the big leagues from collecting the baseball cards. There was a pitcher by the name of Van Lingle Mungo on the Brooklyn team. In our neighborhood, we used to take Major League players' names and use them as our own. So I loved this name, Van Lingle Mungo. From then on, that's all anyone in the town knew me as: Van Lingle Mungo. That was my first recognition of the Dodgers.

I signed with the Philadelphia Phillies in 1945 and was drafted by the Dodgers after the 1948 season. The guy who drafted me, Ed Head, had pitched a no-hit, no-run game for Brooklyn in the big leagues. Ed Head was left-handed but had injured his arm some way when he was growing up. So he turned around and learned how to pitch right-handed.

When I was a minor league player with the Dodgers, the first thing you noticed was the pride within the organization and the desire to win. There were more than 700 minor league ballplayers and 26 minor league teams. I thought there was no way anyone was going to notice me. Branch Rickey ran the minor league system and held Dodger tryout camps throughout the country, always picking up more great players along the way. How he ran 26 farm clubs I'll never know, but the prestigious feeling started in Spring Training when you saw guys like Pee Wee Reese, Gil Hodges, Carl Erskine, Roy Campanella and Jackie Robinson.

We learned in the organization to be proud and to represent that Dodger uniform to the highest degree of class, character and dignity. And when I became the manager, I used to tell people the word *Dodgers* was synonymous with *baseball*. Because if someone said, "I'm with the Padres," you'd say, "When did you become a priest?" If someone said, "I'm with the Twins," you'd say, "Where is your brother or sister?" If someone said, "I'm with the Indians," you'd say, "What reservation are you from?" Or if someone said, "I'm with the Cardinals," you'd say, "Well, the next step is to become the pope." But if you hear the word *Dodgers*, you know they're talking about Major League Baseball. I was the guy who started all those "Dodger Blue" motivational speeches, going back to when I managed in the rookie leagues.

There is tremendous history in the Dodger organization, especially the story of Jackie Robinson. This was someone who established something that was bigger than anyone could imagine when he broke the color barrier when he signed with the Brooklyn organization in 1945. He represented the African-American players and led the way. It wasn't just with baseball, because his success carried great meaning throughout the country and around the world. He was a leader, a competitor and a winner. And I think everyone realizes what a tremendous contribution Jackie Robinson made to the Dodgers and the United States.

I have worn four uniforms in my life that I have been proud to wear: The Boy Scouts of America, the U.S. Army, U.S. Olympic baseball and the Dodgers. I've spent more than six decades with the Dodgers and I have always felt like it is the greatest organization in baseball. At every step in my career I have felt the pride that the Dodgers embody, and have tried to impart that to our fans and players. After managing the Dodgers for 20 years, being inducted into the National Baseball Hall of Fame as a Dodger was more than I ever imagined, and that's pretty good for a skinny left-hander from Norristown who just wanted to pitch like my favorite Dodger.

After the Dodgers clinched the NL West title in San Diego on September 30, 1995, Hall of Famer Tommy Lasorda celebrated with his players in the victorious Dodger clubhouse.

INTRODUCTION
BY **Vin Scully**

In 1936, I was 9 years old and walking home from school, which was 20 blocks from the old Polo Grounds in New York, where Game 2 of the World Series was being played between the Yankees and the Giants. I walked past a Chinese laundry, and posted in the window on a piece of paper was the line score of that World Series game. Until that point, I hadn't really thought much about baseball at all. But when I looked at the final score of the game—Yankees 18, Giants 4—I think that made an impression for two reasons: We were reasonably close to the Polo Grounds, and the "home team" was overwhelmed by the Yankees. So I became a big Giants fan that day at age 9. I guess I was rooting for the underdog.

So that certainly prepared me for working for somewhat of an underdog with the Brooklyn Dodgers. And the first time I was really aware of the Dodgers was two or three years after that 1936 World Series. In either 1938 or 1939, a friend of my mother, a woman, took me to my first game in the bleachers of the Polo Grounds. It cost 55 cents. The doubleheader that we went to see was between the Giants and the Dodgers. And during that game, really, was my first true awareness of the Brooklyn Dodgers.

One of the things that intrigued me about Major League Baseball is the fact that as a youngster, I played a lot of ball. I played in grammar school, and I played varsity ball in high school and varsity ball in college. And I guess if nothing else, I knew how difficult it is to play this game. And then, when I sit in the booth, knowing how difficult it is, I marvel how big league players make it look relatively easy. Another part of the game of baseball is the fact that when you look at a game, each man is clearly defined. He's not hidden; nobody is cutting him off. It's not like football, where he might be buried under six or seven players. They are individually playing with a team effort.

And I guess one of the things I've always loved is that the average baseball fan is absolutely positive that he knows as much as the manager of the baseball team. I think, more than any other sport, the baseball fan truly relates. You can't relate to basketball if you aren't seven feet tall, or to football if you're not a great big guy. But everyone has played some type of baseball or softball. The passion of the game has always intrigued me. I always look forward to coming to the ballpark because of the anticipation about what might happen in the next game.

As far as the Dodger franchise is concerned, in many ways I've often thought that the franchise is somewhat a reflection of life itself. In your early days, you struggle just to pay bills. Eventually, if you're fortunate enough, you might break through and have periods of some success. Along with the success, certainly, as you grow, there is heartache and frustration. But then, the spirit of the borough of Brooklyn has always touched the Dodgers—the idea that, undismayed by the past disappointments, fans will forever cry, "Wait till next year!" So all of that has really helped me feel how important the organization has been to all of baseball, to all the fans and, very much, to me.

Vin Scully was inducted into the National Baseball Hall of Fame in 1982.

CHAPTER

1

Price 5 cents.

Official Score Book

The Brooklyn Base Ball Club Limited

Season of 1890.

WASHINGTON PARK,
5TH AVE. & 4TH ST.

Early Brooklyn
1890–1940

Before They Were the Dodgers

BY RONALD G. SHAFER

As the decade of the 1890s began, Brooklyn, New York teemed with activity as America's fourth-largest city grew to more than 800,000 people. Pedestrians dodged horse-drawn rail cars in the busy streets, while commuters rode elevated trains across the 7-year-old Brooklyn Bridge. Brooklynites united in celebration of their baseball team, which now stood at the pinnacle of the sporting world.

The home team—called the Brooklyn Bridegrooms after several players married just before the 1888 season—had won its first Major League pennant in 1889 in the American Association. More than 353,000 fans had jammed into Washington Park that season, setting a 19th-century record for baseball attendance. Then, just before the 1890 season, Brooklyn transferred into the prestigious National League, the senior circuit of baseball. "Brooklyn is at last in the sphere to which it is most fitted," said *Sporting Life*, "and the general rejoicing in this bailiwick is but what it was natural to expect."

In 1890, however, Brooklyn and all of baseball ran into a buzzsaw. After years of labor unrest, top players revolted and formed a league of their own, the Players' League. The new circuit fielded teams in every National League city, including the Ward's Wonders in Brooklyn, managed by star shortstop John Montgomery "Monte" Ward. Suddenly, three Major Leagues were competing for the affections, and money, of baseball fans.

On the field, the Brooklyn Bridegrooms fared well. While most other National League teams lost star players to the new Players' League, Brooklyn players remained loyal to the club's generous President Charles H. Byrne. In its first year in the National League, Brooklyn won the pennant, becoming the only team in baseball history to win consecutive championships in two different Major Leagues.

Off the field, Brooklyn suffered staggering financial losses, as did nearly all teams that year. Baseball fans, turned off by the bitter quarrelling between the leagues, stayed away in droves. Attendance at Brooklyn Bridegrooms' games in 1890 fell by two-thirds to 121,000, and to survive, the club began looking for new investors.

The Players' League folded after only one season, and the American Association died a year later, leaving the National League as a bloated 12-team monopoly. The owners of the former Players' League Brooklyn Ward's Wonders agreed to become minority investors in the Bridegrooms, but only after two demands were met. First, the Bridegrooms had to move from centrally located Washington Park in South Brooklyn to the Wonders' remote Eastern Park. Second, the Bridegrooms had to hire Monte Ward as manager, forcing out Bill "Gunner" McGunnigle, even though he had led the team to two straight pennants.

Scorebook cover for the 1891 Brooklyn Bridegrooms, who finished 61-76 and sixth in the National League.

Baseball in Brooklyn fell into the doldrums. The team under Ward and then former Bridegrooms star Dave "Needles" Foutz became perennial second-division dwellers. Yearly attendance barely rose above the 200,000 mark as fans shunned Eastern Park. A heavy blow came in early 1898 with the death of the club's visionary president, Byrne, at age 55.

Byrne was one of the founders of the team in 1883 along with newsman George Taylor and two casino owners, Byrne's brother-in-law Joseph Doyle and Ferdinand "Gus" Abell. In 1884, after one minor league season, Byrne took the club into the Major League American Association, with Taylor as the first manager, and built the club into a successful baseball franchise and pennant winner.

The new president was 38-year-old Team Secretary Charles H. Ebbets, whom Byrne had hired in 1883 as a ticket taker and accountant. In an effort to revive the team's fortunes, Ebbets immediately built a new Washington Park in South Brooklyn, across the intersection from the original Washington Park and near rail lines, in time for the 1898 season.

Brooklynites needed a morale boost. In early 1898, the proud, independent city had become a borough of New York City, a decision that many Brooklyn residents now lamented as "the mistake of '98." The new

Washington Park did little to raise spirits. Brooklyn finished a woeful 10th in the National League that year, and as the Spanish-American War overshadowed the country and its favorite pastime, attendance totaled only 123,000 people, the lowest since 1890. The team's recent record, said the *Brooklyn Eagle*, "has been such as to disappoint all patrons of the game who are hoping that the experiences of the future will not be duplicates of the dismal ones of the past."

At this point, 66-year-old Gus Abell, still the team's majority owner, stepped up to the plate. The wealthy Abell previously had been content to stay in the background and bankroll the team. Now he arranged a sensational deal with the owners of the Baltimore Orioles, including its manager, Ned Hanlon, to merge the two teams. The deal brought to Brooklyn future Hall of Famers Hanlon, Wee Willie Keeler and Hughie Jennings.

The deal also generated yet another name for the Brooklyn team, which was still known as the Bridegrooms into the 1890s and as the Trolley Dodgers—and then just Dodgers—because fans had to dodge trolley cars around Eastern Park. With the arrival of manager Hanlon, the team became known as the Superbas after a famous acrobat troupe known as Hanlon's Superbas (though they were of no relation to the Brooklyn manager).

By whatever name, the new team brought baseball excitement back to Brooklyn in 1899. The Superbas easily won Brooklyn's first National League pennant since 1890. Attendance jumped to nearly 270,000 people, the highest since 1889. Fans hailed manager Hanlon as a hero. "You did well, Ned," shouted one enthusiast. "We'll stick to you."

But the fans didn't stick. Even though the Superbas won a second straight pennant in 1900, attendance nosedived below 200,000. One reason was that the new American League raided many of Brooklyn's favorite players. In 1902, Abell, discouraged by the lack of fan support, sold his stock to Charles Ebbets. In 1905, Ebbets became the club's full owner after going into hock to buy out the Baltimore interests to keep the team in Brooklyn.

Ebbets had his work cut out for him. In the early 20th century, America was turning its attention to a broad array of exciting changes. Automobiles were rapidly replacing the horse and buggy. In Dayton, Ohio, the Wright brothers successfully tested a "flying machine." In sports, the game of football was gaining in popularity. Some observers believed that baseball's best years were behind it, but not Ebbets, who saw bigger and better times ahead for the national game. "Baseball is in its infancy," he declared.

Under Ebbets, Brooklyn teams—still called the Superbas—finished no higher than fifth over the next decade. Yet the club managed to draw more than 200,000

THE HANNIS
=WHIS

THEO. BOMEISLER, Sole Agent,
The Hannis Distilling Co. Received the First Prize
in 1876, the New Orleans World's Fair in
Australia in 1887,

DISTILLING CO.
KIES

50 BEAVER ST., NEW YORK.
Medals at the Centennial Exposition in Philadelphia
1885, and the Adelaide Exposition in
over all Competitors.

BROOKLYN.													A B	R	B H	S H	P O	A	E
Batting Order, Position	1	2	3	4	5	6	7	8	9	10	11							
O'Brien, L. F.																		
Collins, 2 B.																		
Foutz, 1 B.																		
Burns, R. F.																		
Pinkney, 3 B.																		
Corkhill, C. F.																		
Visner, C.																		
Caruthers, P.																		
Smith, S. S.																		
Total..																		
Extra Player, Terry.																		

2-Base Hits | 3-Base hits | Home Runs struck Out   Umpire,

ATHLETIC.													A B	R	B H	S H	P O	A	E
Batting Order, Position	1	2	3	4	5	6	7	8	9	10	11							
Welch, C. F.																		
Larkin, 1 B.																		
Lyons, 3 B.																		
Stovey, L. F.																		
Paner, 2 B.																		
Purcell, R. F.																		
Fennelly, S. S.																		
Robinson or Cross, C.																		
Seward or Weyhing, P.																		
Total.....																		
Extra Player, Mattimore.																		

2-Base Hits, | 3-Base Hits, | Home Runs, | struck Out, | Time of Game,

OLD JUDGE CIGARETTES.
GUARANTEED ABSOLUTELY PURE.
GOODWIN & CO.,
NEW YORK.   LONDON.

CLOCKWISE FROM TOP 1889 scorecard; the earliest-known Brooklyn ticket from the 1883 season; 1888 Robert Caruthers baseball card; 1896 Brooklyn Bridegroom admission token for season ticket customers at Eastern Park.

people each year and more than 300,000 twice. Ebbets decided that what was needed to spur bigger interest was a new stadium. He began scouting for land in Brooklyn's Flatbush area in a run-down section known as "Pigtown" because of its garbage dumps. His dummy Pylon Construction Company secretly bought lots there. When Ebbets owned enough land, he announced plans to build a modern, steel-structured baseball stadium.

When the $750,000 price tag of the stadium put a strain on Ebbets' finances, he sold half the club to two old friends, builders Ed and Steve McKeever. At groundbreaking ceremonies in early 1912, Ebbets was still undecided about what to call the new stadium. One newspaper reporter suggested that the baseball man name it after himself, saying "It was your idea and nobody else's."

The Brooklyn club owner didn't need much coaxing. On April 9, 1913, a new era in Brooklyn baseball began with the official opening of Ebbets Field.

Ronald G. Shafer *is the author of* When the Dodgers Were Bridegrooms, *the story of the formation of the franchise that became the Dodgers and the team's first pennants as the Brooklyn Bridegrooms under manager Bill "Gunner" McGunnigle.*

Brooklyn, Nov 20 1889

N. E. Young Esq.
    Pres. and Sec. National League

Dear Sir: I am this day in re-
ceipt of your formal notice of the
fact that The Brooklyn Base Ball
Club was unanimously elected
to membership in the National League
of Professional Base Ball Clubs at
the Annual Meeting of said League
held in NewYork City, Nov 14th.

The Brooklyn Base Ball Club in
accepting such membership desires
to express to the League its sincere
appreciation of the compliment
bestowed upon it and takes plea-
sure in saying, that membership in
a body which for years has struggled
to place the National Game on its

Brooklyn, _____ 18__

present foundation is indeed an honor.

Very Respectfully Yours
CH Byrne
Pres.

Brooklyn, Nov. 20, 1889
N.E. Young Esq.
Pres. and Sec. National League

    Dear Sir: I am this day in receipt of your formal notice of the fact that the Brooklyn Base Ball Club was unanimously elected to membership in the National League of Professional Base Ball Clubs at the Annual Meeting of said League held in New York City, Nov. 14th.
    The Brooklyn Base Ball Club in accepting such membership desires to express to the League its sincere appreciation of the compliment bestowed upon it and takes pleasure in saying that membership in a body which for years has struggled to place the National Game on its present foundation is indeed an honor.

Very Respectfully Yours
CH Byrne
Pres.

Letter from Charles H. Byrne, one of the original founders of the Brooklyn team, accepting membership into the National League.

THE BROOKLYN BALL CLUB
CHARLES H. EBBETS, JR. Secretary.
HENRY W. MEDICUS Treasurer.

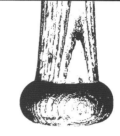

Charles Ebbets

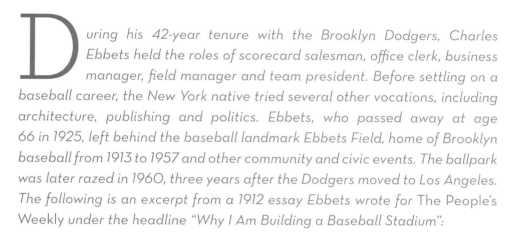

During his 42-year tenure with the Brooklyn Dodgers, Charles Ebbets held the roles of scorecard salesman, office clerk, business manager, field manager and team president. Before settling on a baseball career, the New York native tried several other vocations, including architecture, publishing and politics. Ebbets, who passed away at age 66 in 1925, left behind the baseball landmark Ebbets Field, home of Brooklyn baseball from 1913 to 1957 and other community and civic events. The ballpark was later razed in 1960, three years after the Dodgers moved to Los Angeles. The following is an excerpt from a 1912 essay Ebbets wrote for The People's Weekly under the headline "Why I Am Building a Baseball Stadium":

I am a firm believer in the future of baseball, both in Brooklyn and the country at large. Otherwise I would not invest close to three-quarters of a million dollars in this new park. I want to build a structure that will fill all demands upon it for the next 30 years. . . .

This time we are going to build a permanent steel, brick and cement stadium, which I hope will shelter the Brooklyn club for many years after I have seen my last game. It will seat 25,000 persons and another 10,000 can be accommodated by emergency benches and field space. It will contain every convenience that we can devise and will be absolutely safe. I will no longer have to worry about fires, collapsing stands and other dangers that menace the spectators and of which they seldom give thought.

All these changes have been brought about by the followers of the game. The club owners are but instruments in the hands of the fans. They demand better accommodations, faster play and centrally located parks. They are perfectly willing to pay for these improvements and we must meet their requirements or lose their patronage. The day of twenty-five-cent baseball is past. Every department of the game has

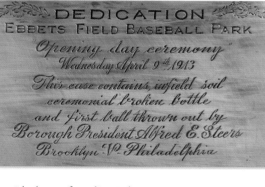

progressed. The players receive salaries that compare favorably with those of any line in business open to the young man of our time. As a result, we get educated, quick-thinking players, physically fit, and the game is decidedly the better for them.

The class of attendance is also higher and the spectators are accustomed to comfort while at work or play. They want the best in baseball and generally get what they want. That's why I am building a new ballpark, situated in the most healthful part of Brooklyn and containing every up-to-date feature. Later I hope the players will capture a pennant, to make the combination complete.

OPPOSITE TOP Presentation box featuring artifacts from the opening of Brooklyn's Ebbets Field in 1913. **OPPOSITE BOTTOM** A vintage pocket mirror with pictures of Charles Ebbets and Henry Medicus. **ABOVE** Dedication plaque from Opening Day Ceremony.

Dazzy Vance

A dvances in modern-day sports medicine and the success of Tommy John surgery in rebuilding the careers of injured pitchers lead to the rueful speculation about Hall of Famers Sandy Koufax and Don Drysdale. Both Los Angeles pitching icons' careers were cut short at relatively young ages in the 1960s, Koufax bowing out at age 30 in 1966 due to arthritis and Drysdale leaving in 1969 at 33 because of a rotator cuff tear.

Back in 1920, Arthur "Dazzy" Vance, a minor league journeyman, accidentally banged his arm on a table during a poker game. The next morning, still inexplicably in pain, he went to the doctor. The diagnosis was an elbow injury that had gone undetected. Vance underwent an elbow surgery that likely relieved the right-hander of bone chips and other loose fragments in his elbow, and at age 29, he suddenly regained his fastball. But Vance needed one more break to begin his epic journey with the Brooklyn Dodgers.

After winning 21 games in 1921 at Class A New Orleans, Vance was offered to Brooklyn in a package deal with highly regarded catcher Hank DeBerry. Dodger Owner Charles Ebbets wanted DeBerry, but he balked at Vance, who owned a lifetime 0-4 Major League record in previous failed auditions with the New York Yankees and the Pittsburgh Pirates. Brooklyn scout Larry Sutton pleaded with Ebbets after hearing DeBerry rave about Vance's talent. Ebbets relented, and Vance earned a spot in the starting rotation the following spring.

For the next seven seasons, Vance led the National League in strikeouts. His fashion trademark was an old undershirt with a tattered right sleeve. Opponents complained about the distracting flannel strips flapping behind his fastball, but Vance claimed it was his "lucky shirt" from New Orleans. The league president couldn't find a rule against tattered shirts, so Vance kept wearing it.

Vance continued pitching in the Majors until age 44. He won 197 games and was elected to the Baseball Hall of Fame in 1955. During his Most Valuable Player Award season in 1924, Vance won the Triple Crown, leading the circuit in victories (28), strikeouts (262) and earned run average (2.16). He won 15 consecutive games that season and set a single-game mark with 15 strikeouts against the Chicago Cubs on August 23.

Also that year, Vance and Burleigh Grimes became the first Dodger teammates to rank Nos. 1 and 2 among National League strikeout leaders—a feat that wouldn't be achieved again until 1960 with a couple of Dodger pitchers named Don Drysdale and Sandy Koufax.

ABOVE Vance led the National League in strikeouts for seven consecutive seasons while with the Brooklyn Dodgers.
OPPOSITE Vance was featured in an advertisement for Celo, a celery-flavored soda popular in the '20s and '30s.

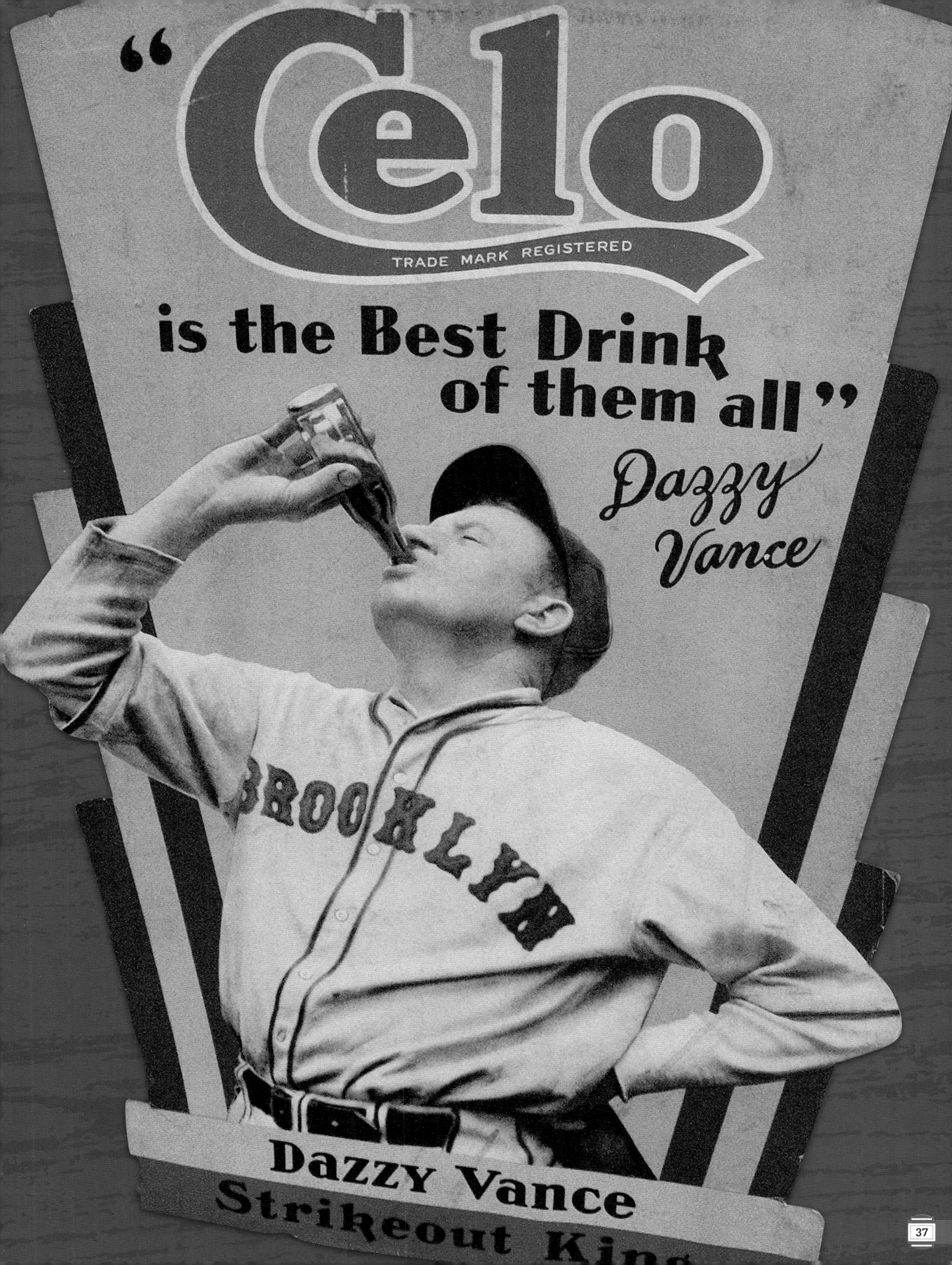
"Celo
TRADE MARK REGISTERED
is the Best Drink
of them all"
Dazzy
Vance
BROOKLYN
Dazzy Vance
Strikeout Kin

Zack Wheat

Team President Charles Ebbets expected an increased player payroll following Brooklyn's 1916 National League pennant and inaugural World Series appearance against the Boston Red Sox. But the salary holdouts of outfielders Hi Myers and Zack Wheat employed different tactics.

Myers had a small farm in Ohio, and he enlisted a friend to print a few sheets of paper with "Myers's Stock Farm" letterhead. Myers wrote Ebbets and said he couldn't afford to return to baseball because of his successful stock farm. Ebbets decided to pay a visit to Myers, who scrambled to keep the charade by "borrowing" herds of cattle and livestock from neighbors to look prosperous. Ebbets fell for the ruse and gave Myers a substantial raise.

Wheat had better leverage and was in the prime of a Hall of Fame career. With Brooklyn from 1909 to 1926, the Missouri native would become the all-time franchise leader in games (2,322), at-bats (8,859), hits (2,804), doubles (464), triples (171) and total bases (4,003). In 1916, Wheat hit .312 and set a Brooklyn record with a 29-game hitting streak.

When Ebbets visited Wheat's home, there were no arguments. Wheat gave Ebbets a "take-it-or-leave-it" offer and then invited the flustered owner to stay for dinner. Ebbets declined and asked for a ride back to the train station.

When Spring Training rolled around, Ebbets and Wheat still were not communicating. Wheat was doing chores on his farm when he received a telegram that stated: "REPORT AT ONCE. C. H. EBBETS."

Arriving at the team's spring hotel, Wheat extended his hand to Ebbets, who said, "It's about time you came to your senses." Wheat was confused and pulled the telegram from his pocket. "This is what brought me here," he said. "Are you trying to go back on your word?" Ebbets cried the telegram was a forgery. The scene attracted a group of sportswriters. One of the writers, Abe Yager, suggested to Ebbets that he find a quiet place to meet with Wheat.

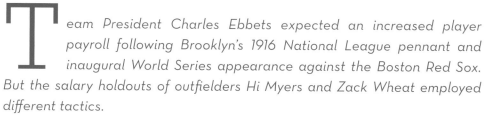

Ebbets agreed and invited Wheat to his room. An hour later, Ebbets announced Wheat had signed his contract but still wondered about the origin of the telegram.

During the summer, when Wheat was again among the league's leading hitters, Yager confessed to Ebbets that he had sent the bogus message.

OPPOSITE ABOVE Zack Wheat's disc from the 1909–1912 Sweet Caporal Domino Discs PX7 set, printed on cardboard with a metal frame.
OPPOSITE & ABOVE Wheat had a trademark style of hitting in a time known as the Dead Ball Era. He held his hands near the end of the bat, which caused a corkscrew type of swing that spiked the ball into the dirt.

Casey Stengel

When New York Yankees rookie outfielder Mickey Mantle visited Brooklyn for the first time during Spring Training in 1951, manager Casey Stengel offered tips on how to read balls that caromed off the right field wall at Ebbets Field.

Mantle stared at his gray-haired mentor with surprise, not realizing he had been a player. "What do you think, I was born at 60?" Stengel cracked.

Stengel earned his Hall of Fame status for his incredible Yankees tenure from 1949 to 1960, in which his Bronx Bombers captured 10 pennants and seven championships in 12 seasons, including five consecutive World Series titles from 1949 to 1953. Stengel had a 4-1 record against Brooklyn in the World Series, winning in 1949, 1952, 1953 and 1956.

Stengel, though, wasn't always a success as manager and often was dismissed as a clown. He piloted Brooklyn from 1934 to 1936, never finishing higher than fifth place, and was fired with one year left on his contract. Stengel didn't win with the Boston Bees/Braves (1938–1943) and ended his career as the wrinkled face of the expansion New York Mets, which went 40-120 in 1962.

As a player, Charles Dillon "Casey" Stengel compiled a lifetime .284 batting average in 14 seasons, the first six with Brooklyn from 1912 to 1917. The Kansas City native (his hometown "K.C." lent him the nickname "Casey") was known both for his sense of humor and his financial acumen. He routinely staged spring holdouts for a higher salary from Brooklyn Owner Charles Ebbets.

With the Pittsburgh Pirates in 1919, Stengel diffused hecklers during a game at Brooklyn with a sparrow hidden in his cap. After walking to the batter's box to a chorus of boos, Stengel tipped his cap. The bird flew away, and Stengel again became a crowd favorite.

In 1924, Stengel married Edna Lawson, and the couple settled in Glendale, California. Edna's father owned a bank, which eventually became the other family business for Casey and his wife besides baseball.

Prior to the first game of the 1957 World Series, Stengel and Milwaukee Braves manager Fred Haney met at home plate for the exchange of lineup cards with umpires. Stengel pointed to Edna in the stands and said to Haney, "She wants to know why you aren't banking with us."

Stengel is the only man to have worn the uniforms of the Brooklyn Dodgers, the New York Giants, the New York Yankees and the New York Mets.

Stengel managed the Brooklyn Dodgers from 1934 to 1936. He is the only man to have worn the uniforms of the Brooklyn Dodgers, the New York Giants, the New York Yankees and the New York Mets.

Bill Terry

The rivalry between the Brooklyn Dodgers and the New York Giants—neighboring teams competing in the same league—produced the predictable clashes among the players and fans of the respective franchises. But an offhand remark during an early-season interview in 1934 by Giants player-manager Bill Terry became a rallying cry for Brooklyn fans.

Asked by a reporter about the Dodgers' pennant chances under first-year manager Casey Stengel, Terry replied, "Is Brooklyn still in the league?"

Under manager Max Carey, the 1933 Dodgers finished in sixth place with a 65-88 record, 26½ games behind the World Series Champion Giants.

Stengel, who played for both the Dodgers and Giants during his playing career, used Terry's quote for motivation during the final week of the 1934 season. Although Brooklyn was heading toward another sixth-place finish, the Dodgers had a chance to ruin the Giants' season. With two games left in the season, the Giants and the St. Louis Cardinals were tied for first place and played at home—the Giants hosted the Dodgers, the Cardinals faced the Cincinnati Reds.

On Saturday, Dodger Van Lingle Mungo scattered five hits in a 5–1 victory over the Giants. Meanwhile, the Cardinals took over first place that afternoon when pitcher Paul "Daffy" Dean defeated the visiting Reds, 6–1, at Sportsman's Park. On Sunday, the Dodgers and the Giants were tied 5–5 after nine innings, but Brooklyn pushed across three runs in the top of the 10th inning against pitchers Hal Schumacher and Carl Hubbell for an 8–5 victory. The Giants were eliminated when the Cardinals blanked the Reds, 9–0, for Jay "Dizzy" Dean's 30th victory of the season. (The Dean brothers played side by side on the Cardinals' roster for several years.) The Giants became the first team to enter September with a seven-game lead and lose the pennant.

Terry's Giants rebounded to win pennants in 1936 and 1937, but the Giants gradually faded from contention. Mel Ott replaced Terry in the dugout when Terry became the team's general manager. Terry lasted one season in the front office and then became a cotton trader in Memphis.

By 1954, Terry owned a Buick dealership in Florida when he was invited to the Dodgers' Spring Training camp in Vero Beach. He spent the day with the team and gave batting tips as the last National League player to hit .400 in a season (.401 with the Giants in 1930). The Dodgers gave Terry the red-carpet treatment. The former nemesis posed in a Dodger uniform by himself and also with Dodger players Jim Gilliam and George Shuba.

The captions from two wire-service photographs that March afternoon were "Terry Turns Turncoat" and "Bill Terry Dons Dodger Uniform."

Bill Terry pictured with Team Secretary Eddie Brannick, *left*, and Treasurer Leo Bondy, *right*.

During the first night game in Ebbets Field history on June 15, 1938, Cincinnati Reds pitcher Johnny Vander Meer pitched his second consecutive no-hitter in a 6–0 victory over the Dodgers.

Larry MacPhail

U sually a hurricane leaves behind a trail of destruction, but the turbulent five-year reign of Brooklyn Dodger President Larry MacPhail actually provided a solid foundation to a teetering franchise. After rebuilding the Cincinnati Reds from 1934 to 1937, MacPhail answered the emergency call from the Brooklyn Trust Company. His formula of expanding the operating budget to acquire quality players and implementing creative marketing ideas transformed the Dodgers from laughingstock to pennant contenders.

Before MacPhail arrived in Brooklyn, the Brooklyn Dodgers, the New York Giants and the New York Yankees had signed a five-year agreement to prevent radio broadcasts, fearing attendance would drop if fans could hear the games in their homes. MacPhail scoffed at the arrangement and hired his play-by-play announcer from Cincinnati, Red Barber.

With the Reds and the Dodgers, MacPhail was the first to introduce the Major Leagues to night baseball, televised games, Old-Timers' games featuring former players, airplane travel for baseball teams, a stadium club lounge, season-ticket plans, batting helmets and regularly scheduled doubleheaders.

MacPhail was on his way to becoming a Hall of Fame executive, a remarkable feat considering he didn't start in baseball until age 40. As a youth, the Michigan native became business savvy by watching his father set up a chain of banks across the country. At age 20, he earned his law degree. After a brief law career, MacPhail took turns operating a tool company and clothing store.

During World War I, MacPhail enlisted in the 114th Field Artillery and rose to the rank of captain. When the war ended, MacPhail plotted with six others to sneak into Holland and kidnap the former Kaiser of Germany, Wilhelm II, who had sought refuge at Amerongen. They stormed the castle but called off the plan when a suspicious sentry sounded the alarm. Before departing, MacPhail swiped an ashtray off the kaiser's desk, which became a proud souvenir and popular story at Brooklyn's Ebbets Field.

ABOVE On his last day with the Dodgers in 1942, Brooklyn Dodger President Larry MacPhail received a watch from Dolph Camilli on behalf of the Brooklyn players and coaches. **OPPOSITE** MacPhail provided a teetering franchise with a solid foundation. He outlined the Dodgers' accomplishments in this letter to fans.

BROOKLYN NATIONAL LEAGUE BASEBALL CLUB

Dodgers

OFFICES
215 MONTAGUE ST.

BROOKLYN, NEW YORK

GAMES AT
EBBETS FIELD

L. S. MacPHAIL, PRESIDENT

December 16, 1940

DEAR DODGER FANS:

As the year draws to a close I would like to take this opportunity to tell you something of the accomplishments of your ball club during the past three seasons.

Since Opening Day, 1938, over 2,800,000 people have paid their way into Ebbets Field. These admissions have formed the cornerstone on which we have been able to erect a baseball structure which we believe is sound, and will enable Brooklyn to have a contending ball club in the National League over a long period.

Over one million dollars has been expended during the past three years to improve the playing personnel. At least $750,000 has been for players who came directly to the Dodgers; six players (Medwick, Higbe, Owen, Camilli, Reese and Wyatt) having necessitated an outlay of almost a half million dollars, while the balance has been spent in the development of young players and in our farm clubs.

More than $250,000 has gone into the improvement of Ebbets Field which, although built in 1912, is now a modern, comfortable ball park with all the facilities of a present day stadium. Our lighting system is regarded as the best in baseball.

During this period not one cent has been taken out of the club by any stockholder and all profits have been put back into the club for the benefit of Brooklyn and its baseball fans. You have made this picture possible and we recognize our obligation to you--the faithful fans who support the club.

Our main object is to bring a pennant and a World's Championship to Brooklyn and all the efforts of our entire organization are directed toward that goal.

The Directors, Stockholders, Leo Durocher, all of the players and our entire organization join with me in wishing you all a very Merry Christmas and a prosperous New Year.

Cordially,

Larry MacPhail

Leo Durocher

Leo Durocher and Larry MacPhail never backed down from a fight, which always caused fireworks when they turned on each other. And the two most famous confrontations during their respective Brooklyn Dodger tenures started for reasons unbeknownst to Durocher.

In 1939 MacPhail, as Brooklyn Dodger team president, hatched a secret deal with Branch Rickey of the St. Louis Cardinals. Major League Baseball had declared 74 players in the St. Louis farm system free agents because Rickey was trying to control the flow of amateur talent. The only player Rickey hated to lose was outfielder Pete Reiser.

The Dodgers signed Reiser and were supposed to keep him "hidden" in the low minors until 1940, when Rickey could reacquire him via trade. A rookie manager in 1939, Durocher didn't know about the deal, so he started to play the 19-year-old Reiser in Spring Training. In three exhibition games against the Cardinals, Reiser reached base in 11 consecutive plate appearances, including seven hits and four home runs. Durocher soon received a cryptic telegram from MacPhail that stated: *"DO NOT PLAY REISER AGAIN."*

Durocher wrote Reiser's name in the lineup again and was summoned to MacPhail's hotel suite. MacPhail fired Durocher and unleashed a tirade of expletives and insults. Durocher pushed his boss, who fell over the bed in a somersault. When MacPhail stood up, he smiled and told Durocher he still was the manager but that Reiser needed further seasoning in the minor leagues. The Dodgers called off the Reiser deal. He was sent to Brooklyn's Class A Elmira affiliate in 1939 and two years later won the National League batting title.

The other big fight between Durocher and MacPhail occurred the day the Dodgers clinched the pennant in 1941. Preparing for their team's first World Series appearance since 1920, Brooklyn fans eagerly assembled at New York's Grand Central Terminal to meet the train arriving from Boston. Durocher heard some players wanted to get off at the second-to-last stop, the 125th Street station, to avoid the large crowds.

Durocher ordered the train to proceed directly to Grand Central without stopping. He didn't realize MacPhail and Rickey were standing on the 125th Street platform, waiting to board the train to congratulate the Dodger players. When the trained breezed past MacPhail, he assumed Durocher had snubbed him on purpose. That evening, MacPhail fired Durocher.

Durocher retreated to his room in utter dejection. On the eve of facing the New York Yankees, Durocher's dream had turned into a nightmare. A manager had never before been dismissed before a World Series.

The next morning, MacPhail called Durocher and asked him to stop by his office. Durocher grumbled something about a severance check and hung up the phone. When he walked into the office, MacPhail was smiling and wearing a blue suit with a fresh carnation in his lapel.

"Guess I got a little out of line last night," MacPhail said. "Pull up a chair, and we'll figure out how to beat those Yankees."

OPPOSITE Manager Leo Durocher, *right*, with coach Charlie Dressen, who later piloted Brooklyn from 1951 to 1953.

EARLY BROOKLYN

49

Babe Ruth

"**W**hen did Babe Ruth play for the Dodgers?" The most frequent question during tours of modern-day Dodger Stadium occurs when fans notice the sport's most familiar face wearing a "B" cap and the "Dodgers" script. The simple answer is: Ruth was a coach during the 1938 season and wore uniform No. 35.

But George Herman "Babe" Ruth's bittersweet tenure in Brooklyn was a complicated mix of publicity and politics. The reigning home run king had been out of baseball since his retirement as a player from the Boston Braves in 1935. First-year Dodger President Larry MacPhail signed Ruth in June 1938 to generate publicity for a Brooklyn team languishing in the standings. Ruth saw an opportunity to perhaps manage the Dodgers in 1939 if the embattled Burleigh Grimes, who had clashed with his new boss during Spring Training, didn't return.

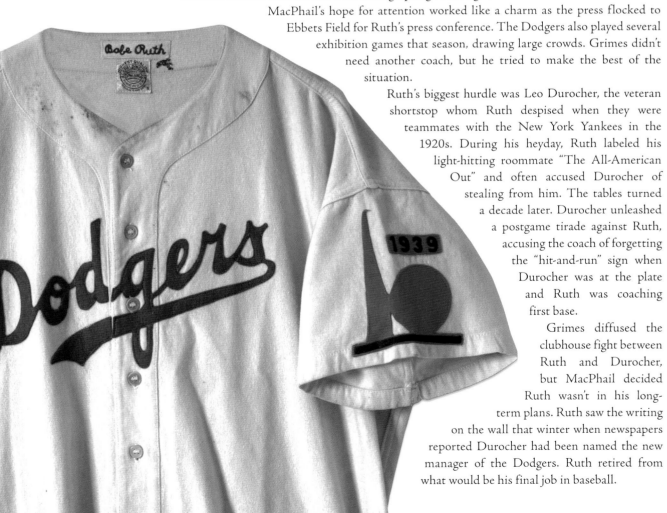

MacPhail's hope for attention worked like a charm as the press flocked to Ebbets Field for Ruth's press conference. The Dodgers also played several exhibition games that season, drawing large crowds. Grimes didn't need another coach, but he tried to make the best of the situation.

Ruth's biggest hurdle was Leo Durocher, the veteran shortstop whom Ruth despised when they were teammates with the New York Yankees in the 1920s. During his heyday, Ruth labeled his light-hitting roommate "The All-American Out" and often accused Durocher of stealing from him. The tables turned a decade later. Durocher unleashed a postgame tirade against Ruth, accusing the coach of forgetting the "hit-and-run" sign when Durocher was at the plate and Ruth was coaching first base.

Grimes diffused the clubhouse fight between Ruth and Durocher, but MacPhail decided Ruth wasn't in his long-term plans. Ruth saw the writing on the wall that winter when newspapers reported Durocher had been named the new manager of the Dodgers. Ruth retired from what would be his final job in baseball.

LEFT First base coach Babe Ruth wore uniform No. 35 with the Dodgers in 1938. **OPPOSITE** Cover of the Dodger scorecard from 1938.

BROOKLYN DODGERS
VS
SYRACUSE CHIEFS

5^c

5^c

SOUVENIR SCORECARD

Red Barber

A Major League broadcaster with the Cincinnati Reds (1934-1938), the Brooklyn Dodgers (1939-1953) and the New York Yankees (1954-1966), Walter Lanier "Red" Barber was brought to Brooklyn when Dodger President Larry MacPhail decided to end the five-year agreement among the three New York teams not to broadcast games on the radio. Barber became one of the most popular personalities in team history. When Branch Rickey succeeded MacPhail, he confided to Barber his desire to integrate baseball. In a 1977 interview with Vin Scully at Dodger Stadium, Barber recalled the events surrounding Rickey and Jackie Robinson:

Mr. Rickey was a very thoughtful man. Before he even knew Jackie Robinson existed, he made up his mind in principle that he was going to break the color line. I was the broadcaster in Brooklyn and I think I was a person of some substance. Mr. Rickey understood that and also knew I was born in Mississippi and grew up in central Florida. He understood that I had better get myself straightened out or he would have to find another announcer. And he had to find out in plenty of time. So one day he told me at lunch what he was going to do. My immediate reaction was going home that night and telling my wife, Lylah, that I was quitting. Then a few days went by and I began to understand that I had the best broadcasting job in sports. And then a little more time went by and I was thinking, "What choice did I have to the parents I was born to?" I didn't know Jackie Robinson then, but what choice did a black man have to his parents? Well, that humbled me a great bit.

They say there isn't anything as compelling as the voice from the grave. I remember what Commissioner Landis said before the first World Series I was on in 1935. In those days, there were no exclusive broadcasts, so all the networks were there. All the announcers met with Landis and it made a great impression on my life.

Landis said, "Gentlemen, I'm not going to tell you how to do your work—you're the best in your business. But this afternoon, there are going to be two teams on the field and they are the best in their business. Don't you try to play ball—you report what the ballplayers do and have no opinions about it. And there are going to be two managers. You probably won't see them because they will be in the dugout. But they will make decisions—don't have an opinion on their decisions; just report their decisions. There are going to be four umpires out there; you'll see them. For goodness sake, don't you have an opinion about their decisions. You are to report everything you can see. Suppose a ballplayer decides to come over to my box and spit tobacco in my face. Don't have an opinion about a ballplayer spitting in the commissioner's face. Just report what he does, report the accuracy, and velocity and the amount, if your eyes are sharp enough. Just report the reaction of the commissioner, if he has one."

Well, the voice from the grave as I was trying to wrestle in my mind about a black man coming to Brooklyn, before we knew it would be Robinson, I said to myself, "It's so easy. I'm not Mr. Rickey. I'm not the players or the manager. I'm not a sociologist. I'm a broadcaster. All I'm to do is report." That's all I ever did.

OPPOSITE Broadcaster Red Barber was elected to the Baseball Hall of Fame in 1978. **ABOVE** Drink coasters featured advertisement for Barber's television show, sponsored by the Feigenspan brewing company.

CHAPTER

2

Brooklyn's Golden Era
1941–1957

The Shrine: Not Camelot, but Ebbets Field

BY ROGER KAHN

When youngsters ask these days what it was like following the Brooklyn Dodgers long ago, I first report that way back then on Flatbush Avenue, many a T. Rex roared and rumbled. That made it awfully tough to cross the street toward Ebbets Field.

A little hyperbole illuminates the imagination. In truth the dinosaurs were gone from Brooklyn then, but what did screech and clatter for the great length of Flatbush Avenue were trolley cars, rolling on iron wheels on iron tracks. In the magical world of long-ago Brooklyn, trolley cars seemed to be everywhere: on Flatbush and Vanderbilt Avenues, on Empire Boulevard, on Fulton Street. As you may have surmised, those noisy cars led to one of the greatest of team nicknames. To survive in Brooklyn, Manhattan folk said haughtily, you had to know how to dodge trolleys. Somewhere along, about 1885, a forgotten poet nicknamed the Brooklyn ballclub "The Trolley Dodgers." Other nicknames came and went. The trolleys themselves vanished (along with the dinosaurs). The core of the nickname, the Dodgers, remained.

During the 1930s, riding a trolley was basic to getting to a Dodger game. I remember clutching my father's hand as we climbed aboard the Tompkins Avenue trolley then riding along for 20 minutes or so, getting closer, ever closer, to the shrine. Strangers began talking baseball with us. The sun was bright. I was going to a Dodger game with my dad. That may be as much of heaven as I shall know.

The ballclub we were to see was no powerhouse. A reporter for *The New York Sun* summed up Dodger teams of the mid-1930s with a droll comment from Spring Training in Clearwater, Florida. "Overconfidence," wrote Eddie Murphy, "may cost the Dodgers fifth place."

Back then, the New York Yankees and the New York Giants dominated both the New York area and the pennant races. Jimmy Cannon, a fine columnist who grew up in Greenwich Village, liked to point out that the Giants, going back to John McGraw and Christy Mathewson, were the original New York team. The Yankees of Babe Ruth and Lou Gehrig arrived two decades later. "Real New Yorkers," Cannon told me, "root for the Giants. The Yankees are strictly for tourists."

But in Brooklyn we took great pride in our second-division club. We had a few splendid ballplayers, Jersey Joe Stripp at third and the mighty fireballer Van Lingle Mungo. Brooklyn was a borough, not a city, but we had our own big league team. Think of all the full-fledged cities that did not.

My father, Gordon Jacques Kahn, had played college ball, and at his side in Ebbets Field I got a solid grounding in the game. On pitching: "Speed alone is not enough."

PREVIOUS An estimated one million fans jammed downtown Brooklyn on September 29, 1941 for a parade prior to the Dodgers' first World Series appearance in 21 years. **OPPOSITE** The Brooklyn Dodgers called Ebbets Field home from 1913 to 1957.

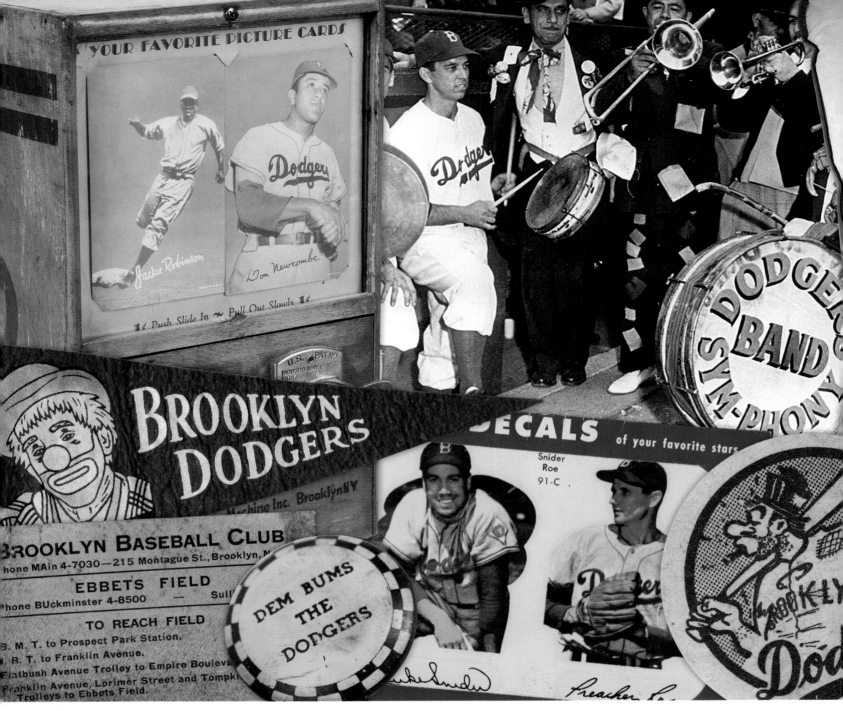

Dodger memorabilia from the team's Brooklyn era at Ebbets Field.

On the caliber of play: "There are no bad ballplayers in the Major Leagues." On eating during a game: "You may have one hot dog, not two. Your mother is concerned that a second hot dog will spoil your appetite for dinner."

With a few more years, I began going to games with teammates from the Froebel Academy baseball team. Froebel is gone today, a victim of urban change, but the chairman of its board of trustees is well remembered. His name: Walter Francis O'Malley. Yes, *that* Walter O'Malley, in the very substantial flesh.

If we had the cash, we paid our way in. If we lacked the $1.10 that general admission tickets cost, we lay down on the sidewalk alongside Bedford Avenue and peered underneath the enormous exit gate that did not quite reach the ground. Lying there you could see

(for free) everything but right field. The hazards were wind, which blew clusters of dirt into your eyes, and the police. Occasionally a cop jabbed us with his nightstick and growled in police Brooklynese, "Gerrada here." We fled, of course, but at a safe distance shouted at our blue tormentor, "Weren't you ever a kid yourself?"

Ebbets Field could hold about 33,000 fans. (Capacity varied with the number of fire department inspectors the Dodger management chose to bribe.) The acoustics were so good that you could hear the players chattering during infield drills. One well-known fan was a beefy lady named Hilda Chester, who sat in the lower deck in center and before each game bellowed at the Dodgers' slim young shortstop, "Pee Wee, have you had your glass of milk today?" Reese, an unfailingly courteous man, always

stopped practice and called back to center field, "Yes, Hilda. I've had my glass of milk."

The Ebbets Field public address announcer, Tex Rickards, was famous for unusual turns of phrase. One day he said over the loudspeakers, "Attention, please. A child has been found lost!"

And one of my favorite bits of baseball humor was spoken quietly. Preacher Roe, a wondrous left-hander, was pitching to Stan Musial when suddenly he called in Duke Snider from center field.

"Do you want me to play deeper?" Snider said.

"No," said Preacher. "Higher."

Of course the grandest accomplishment in Brooklyn came with Jackie Robinson and the integration of baseball. I don't believe America could have made its great journey from Jim Crow to Barack Obama without Jack's gifts and boundless courage.

In 1953 he asked me to help him start a magazine called *Our Sports*, aimed at African-American fans. That led to a friendship that remains one of the glories of my life. Jack died at only 53, and when he knew the end was coming, he wrote a stirring epitaph: "A life is not important except in the impact it has on other lives."

Those words are carved into Jackie's gravestone in Cypress Hills Cemetery, which lies in his adopted borough.

I hope that stone, like all these vibrant Brooklyn memories, endures forever.

Roger Kahn *is the author of 19 books, including* The Boys of Summer, *about growing up near Ebbets Field and the Brooklyn Dodgers.*

ENTER GATE

SEC. ROW SE

37 13 9

LOWER STA
RESERVED SEAT

WORLD SERIES
1952 Dodgers

NATIONAL LEAGUE vs.
AMERICAN LEAGUE
EBBETS FIELD

RAIN CHECK
THIS CHECK

NOT GOOD IF DET

FIELD SERIES
52
L LEAGUE
N LEAGUE
STAND
ED SEAT
included)

SEC.
131

LOWER STAND

1953 WORLD SERIES
EBBETS FIELD
Dodgers

SEAT

38

ES. SEAT S

DODGERS VS YANKEES

RAIN CHECK · RETAIN THIS CHECK · NOT GOOD IF DETACHED

GAME 4

LOWER STAND · RES. SEAT · $7.00

GAME 4

ENTER GATE E

SEC.	ROW	SEAT
28	17	17

LOWER STAND RES. SEAT $7.35

Dodgers

EBBETS FIELD

1955 WORLD SERIES

NATIONAL LEAGUE vs AMERICAN LEAGUE

RAIN CHECK · RETAIN THIS CHECK · NOT GOOD IF DETACHED

ADMIT ONE—SUBJECT TO THE CONDITIONS SET FORTH ON THE BACK HEREOF.

PLAYED UNDER THE SUPERVISION OF

Ford C. Frick
Commissioner of Baseball

GAME 5

LOWER STAND $7.35

GAME 5

DO NOT DETACH · THIS COUPON FROM · RAIN CHECK

Branch Rickey

*I*f winning a championship was his primary benchmark for success, Branch Rickey may never have left the St. Louis Cardinals after the team's 1942 World Series triumph. But the move to the Brooklyn Dodgers, also assisted by a personality conflict with St. Louis Owner Sam Breadon, gave Rickey the opportunity to challenge a haunting memory from the past.

In 1904, Rickey was a student coach at Ohio Wesleyan University when his team traveled to the University of Notre Dame. Rickey's party started to register at the Oliver Hotel in South Bend, Indiana, but the clerk stopped the team's only black player, a catcher named Charles Thomas. The clerk suggested Thomas stay at the local YMCA. Rickey tried to move the entire team to the YMCA but found out there were no rooms.

Thomas offered to go back to Ohio Wesleyan, but Rickey made a deal with the hotel manager for Thomas to stay in his room until a suitable black family could be found. Rickey then called for a cot and announced Thomas wasn't going anywhere.

Inside Rickey's room, Thomas began crying and rubbing his hands. Rickey never forgot the lament of Thomas: "Black skin, black skin. If only I could only rub it off and make it white."

Rickey said, "Tommy, the day will come when they don't have to be white."

After joining the Dodgers, Rickey met with the team's board of directors and discussed his plans for "mass scouting—and that might include a Negro player or two." The directors, which included George McLaughlin of the Brooklyn Trust Company and future Dodger President Walter O'Malley, approved Rickey's plans and pledged their secrecy.

Needing a cover story, Rickey hatched a convenient diversion by announcing he was organizing a "United States League" to compete with the existing Negro American and National Leagues. Rickey was going to field a team, the "Brown Dodgers," which was to play in Ebbets Field when the Brooklyn Dodgers were on the road. Now, Rickey could send scouts like Wid Matthews, George Sisler, Clyde Sukeforth and Tom Greenwade to look for Negro players. All the scouts, with the exception of Greenwade, thought they were looking for players for the "Brown Dodgers."

Eventually Rickey received multiple scouting reports in 1945 on a 26-year-old shortstop with the Kansas City Monarchs named Jackie Robinson who had been a multisport star at UCLA, served in the military and was discharged with the rank of lieutenant.

Rickey dispatched Sukeforth, a former Major League catcher, to Chicago on a special assignment. The Monarchs were scheduled to play the Chicago American Giants, but Robinson was out of the lineup with a slight injury. Sukeforth convinced Robinson to secretly travel to New York but didn't give any details of Rickey's plans. On August 28, 1945, Sukeforth escorted Robinson to the Brooklyn Dodger offices on 215 Montague Street. When he saw Robinson at his office door, Rickey said, "Come in, come in!"

OPPOSITE Branch Rickey was a reserve catcher with the St. Louis Browns and the New York Highlanders from 1905 to 1907.
ABOVE Jackie Robinson and Branch Rickey at the October 23, 1945 signing of Robinson's historic contract.

The War Years

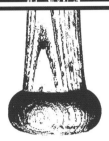

W hen the United States entered World War II following the attack on Pearl Harbor in December 1941, Commissioner Kenesaw Landis wasn't sure that Major League Baseball should proceed with the 1942 season. President Franklin Roosevelt's "Green Light Letter" to Commissioner Landis expressed the importance of baseball during wartime and quelled the commissioner's concerns.

Admitting it was his personal opinion and that the decision of whether to play rested with Landis and the ballclub owners, Roosevelt wrote, "I honestly feel that it would be best for the country to keep baseball going. There will be fewer people unemployed and everybody will work longer and harder than ever before. And that means they ought to have a chance for recreation and for taking their minds off work even more than before. . . . Even if the actual quality to the teams is lowered by the greater use of older players, this will not dampen the popularity of the sport."

Adopting the country's "V for Victory" campaign, Brooklyn's Ebbets Field sported a huge V symbol on the park wall in red, white and blue. Each of the panels of the marble rotunda entrance featured Vs encircled by blue stars. Throughout the park, the upright girders were divided into

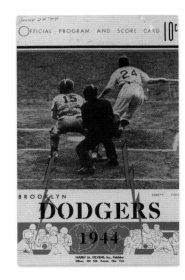

red, white and blue sections, with the white center section decorated with a V. The seats were painted blue and the railings red, carrying out the V theme throughout the grandstands.

Ballparks across the country staged war bond rallies and other patriotic-themed programs and exhibitions. During the war, fat was used to make explosives, so there were occasional "Fat Days" at Ebbets Field, on which any fan who brought a container of fat to the ballpark would receive free admission. If a foul ball was hit into the grandstands, patrons were asked to return them to a receptacle by the dugout so they could be distributed to service units. The lyrics to the national anthem were printed in the Dodger programs so fans could sing along with ballpark organist Gladys Goodding.

On June 26, 1944, the Brooklyn Dodgers, the New York Giants and the New York Yankees played a three-sided game at the Polo Grounds. In the round-robin format, each team sat out for a full inning and then played for two consecutive innings. The war bond fund-raising event featured contests for the longest drive hit by a fungo bat (won by 18-year-old Brooklyn pitcher Cal McLish), throwing accuracy for catchers and a sprint in which one runner started at home and the other at second base. Comedian Milton Berle introduced musical acts, and former New York Mayor Jimmy Walker gave the lineup of some former New York–based stars, including Herb Pennock, Zack Wheat, Nap Rucker, Hooks Wiltse and Roger Bresnahan. The event raised more than $6.5 million in war bond sales.

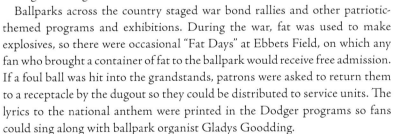

ABOVE & OPPOSITE During World War II, Ebbets Field adopted the country's "V for Victory" campaign and Dodger publications featured a list of players who served in the military.

odgers in Service

1944

EY
TLEY
RGE
MPANIS
CASEY
E CORBITT
FF DAPPER
FALZONE
RRY FRENCH
ACK GRAHAM

JOE HATTEN

KIRBY HIGBE

GIL HODGES

CHET KEHN

DON PADGETT

HAROLD REESE

PETE REISER

LEW RIGGS

JOHN RIZZO

STAN ROJEK

HERMAN FRANKS
CHRIS HAUGHEY
GENE HERMANSKI
HARRY LAVAGETTO

OOKLYN
odgers
FR POST

Latest Picture of "Pistol Pete"

HAROLD REISER

Despite the fine play of Augie Galan in centerfield for the Dodgers this season, Brooklyn fans will always remember the kid who came from "nowhere" to win acclaim and fame as the youngest player ever to wear the National League batting championship crown.

When they think of "Pete" Reiser they will think of home runs smashed to win crucial games . . . they will think of a sturdy young man racing, jumping, diving to make brilliant defensive plays as he roamed his position in centerfield. And they will think of that waning afternoon in St. Louis in 1942 when that fighting Reiser spirit . . . that will to win . . . led him to crash into a concrete wall in a valiant attempt to thwart the "enemy."

Truly, if Pete Reiser is representative of the young American men in uniform, victory must certainly be ours.

Giants *vs* Dodgers *vs* Yanks

TRI-CORNERED BASEBALL GAME
Presented by War Bond Sports Committee
FIFTH WAR LOAN
P LO GROUNDS ★ MONDAY, JUNE 26, 1944

DODGERS
CLUB HOUSE

KEEP OUT

Jackie Robinson

I *nfielder Jackie Robinson (1919–1972) broke baseball's color barrier with the Brooklyn Dodgers in 1947. The six-time All-Star spent his entire 10-year career with the Dodgers, opting to retire instead of accepting a trade to the New York Giants in January 1957. Robinson was selected Rookie of the Year in 1947, an award that today bears his name, and NL Most Valuable Player in 1949. When Sport magazine celebrated its 25th anniversary in 1971, it named Robinson the most "significant" athlete of the previous quarter century. Robinson spoke to respected baseball historian Ted Patterson about that recognition:*

The most significant athlete award is related to a great deal more than my performance on the field. It does have much to do with what happened on the playing field, but it also says that a man can be rewarded for standing up for his convictions and must have meaning to all those who played a part in making a difficult task much, much easier. There were certainly those who did not want us to succeed, but for every one of them there were hundreds that were rooting for our success. . . .

I heard many things that happened on the playing field, but the things that I didn't hear about, the pressures from family and friends, must have been tremendous on those players who cared. There were many incidents that could prove my point. Some eased away, others caused many problems. But there is one that stands out in my mind, one that was a simpler gesture, but with tremendous meaning. Back in 1948, as we took our positions for infield practice, some Boston players figured that Pee Wee Reese, a southerner, would react to their taunts about playing alongside of me on the Dodgers. There wasn't the viciousness as there was with the taunts of Ben Chapman and some of the Phillies, but it was strong enough. Well, Reese did react. He left his shortstop position, came over to me at second base, placed his arms on my shoulder and said something. I don't remember the words and I'm sure Pee Wee doesn't remember either. But his actions had great meaning. The heckling stopped and the bench cleared in no time. Pee Wee Reese by his gesture said simply, "Yell and scream all you like. We're a team. We came to play ball together." Because of attitudes like that, we were able to win six pennants in 10 years. And while we were able to conquer the Yankees only once in those six tries, I think we made our mark on them, and on the game and on the nation. And I can't help feeling if Americans today would take a page out of Pee Wee Reese's book, if we could develop this kind of understanding in today's troubled world, how much further along as a nation we would be.

OPPOSITE After his contract was purchased by the Dodgers, Jackie Robinson posed for a final time in his Montreal uniform during the spring of 1947. **OPPOSITE BOTTOM** Jackie Robinson mechanical tabletop game, circa 1955. **ABOVE** Robinson's No. 42 was retired by Major League Baseball in 1997.

Walter O'Malley

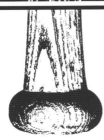

A s the legal counsel of the Brooklyn Dodgers, Walter O'Malley wrote a letter on October 14, 1946, to Emil Praeger, a distinguished Navy captain who developed the original design of the concrete floating breakwater during World War II. Praeger, who was in charge of all engineering projects for the Department of Parks in New York City, also played major roles designing the renovation of the White House and the Los Angeles Public Library.

Of a potential new ballpark in Brooklyn, O'Malley wrote: "They say everything happens in Brooklyn, but here is something that didn't. Your fertile imagination should have some ideas about enlarging or replacing our current stadium . . ."

O'Malley became team president in September 1950. And while the team was successful on the field, O'Malley kept his eye on the grandstands. Though considered cozy and part of the neighborhood landscape since its opening in 1913, Ebbets Field had limited seating capacity and lacked any significant parking lots, so it wasn't part of O'Malley's grand vision.

O'Malley had worked with Praeger on the construction of a 5,000-seat facility at the Dodgers' Spring Training headquarters in Vero Beach, Florida. Holman Stadium opened in 1953 and

was the first major improvement to the land, which was formerly home to a naval air station. The project also gave O'Malley confidence in Praeger for the next ballpark project, wherever it might be.

After consecutive World Series appearances in 1952 and 1953, the cover of the Dodgers' 1954 yearbook featured Willard Mullin's "Brooklyn Bum" cartoon character dreaming of a modern ballpark. Winning pennants wasn't going to secure the team a new park, however, and O'Malley grew frustrated when negotiations with city officials stalled. The National League Braves had moved their franchise from Boston to Milwaukee in 1953 and experienced a boom in home attendance, sweetening the prospect of a similar move to a new city for the Dodgers.

When the Dodgers clinched the 1956 pennant during the final weekend of the season, O'Malley appeared on the television postgame show. Amid the shouting and celebration in the clubhouse, O'Malley reminded everyone about wanting to build a new sports venue in Brooklyn.

The handwriting appeared on the wall in the spring of 1957 when the Dodgers purchased the Pacific Coast League's Los Angeles Angels franchise from Chicago Cubs Owner Phil Wrigley. The acquisition also included the territorial rights to the Southern California market, which gave O'Malley an option to move the team there in case nothing could be worked out back in New York. The Dodgers would spend the 1957 season in Brooklyn, as O'Malley needed to let the process work out on both coasts.

During a Spring Training interview with a Los Angeles radio reporter, O'Malley was asked about the chances of a Brooklyn ballpark being built. "Well, there are some very sincere people working on it," he said. "Of course they've been working on it for a long, long time."

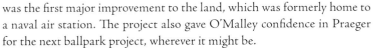
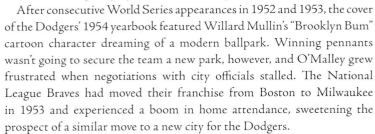

ABOVE The 1954 Dodger yearbook cover featured the Brooklyn Bum by cartoonist Willard Mullin dreaming of a new Brooklyn ballpark. **OPPOSITE** Walter O'Malley with Team Vice Presidents Buzzie Bavasi, *left*, and Red Patterson, *right*.

Milwaukee Braves versus Brooklyn Dodgers, June 17, 1956.

MEMBERSHIP CARD — 1952
This is to certify that

is a bonafide member of
LOEW'S THEATRES AND M-G-M PICTURES
HAPPY FELTON
"KNOT-HOLE GANG"

NATIONAL PRESIDENT

Nᵒ 9328

THE HAPPY FELTON KNOT-HO

I promise to Keep in good condi
quit while giving Only my best i
of sportsmanship.
To give a Helping hand to On
teammates and to Live cleanly Ev
God grant me a strong body A
and the will to Never Gripe abo
and still try my best to win.

The Knothole Gang

BY CHARLEY STEINER

At the age of 7, I had two childhood dreams. Improbably I accomplished one but struck out on the other. I wanted to be the Brooklyn Dodgers' announcer. Just as desperately, I wanted to appear on Happy Felton's Knothole Gang, a 15-minute pregame show that aired on WOR-TV prior to afternoon games at Ebbets Field from the right field corner, where the Dodger bullpen was situated.

Francis "Happy" Felton and his show were reflective of a less complicated and more innocent (dare I say happier) time and place. The premise was simple: three kids dressed in their woolen Little League uniforms and caps would take fungoes, learn how to grip a curveball, and play catch with and run for one of their Dodger heroes, who would in turn briefly teach the fundamentals of the game.

What kid wouldn't want to meet Duke or Pee Wee or Campy or Jackie, much less learn the game from one of their idols? The boys would show off their skills, and then one would be anointed the winner and awarded a brand-new glove. Not just any glove, mind you, but a Rawlings Major League glove. This was a very big deal.

Happy was a larger-than-life personality who weighed close to 300 pounds and wore pronounced horn-rimmed eyeglasses. On the small black-and-white antenna-aided television screen, his smile was seemingly as large as he was. His nickname, "Happy," was pitch-perfect. Now, remember, in 1950, when Felton took his *Knothole Gang* idea to Branch Rickey, there weren't very many pregame shows on the air of any kind, much less any instructional ones. Its brilliance was its simplicity. The man who gave us Jackie Robinson also gave us Happy Felton.

As the story goes, prior to the very first *Knothole Gang* telecast, Happy and the first three contestants were on the field, the kids wearing their Little League uniforms, Felton in street clothes and a Brooklyn cap. Umpire Babe Pinelli (who six years later called the third strike on Dale Mitchell, completing Don Larsen's perfect game) instructed Felton that in the future, only uniformed personnel were permitted on the field. The next day, the Dodgers found Felton a uniform, no easy task for such a, well, rotund fellow. From that day on, Happy Felton became a fixture on Dodger home telecasts, including a postgame show called *Talk to the Stars*, which the players received a fat 50 bucks for an appearance.

But it was the *Knothole Gang* that young (now old) Dodger fans, who grew up in a different time and place, remember most fondly. When the Dodgers left after the 1957 season, Felton stayed in Brooklyn, where memories of his show remain Happy ones.

New York native **Charley Steiner,** *a Dodger broadcaster since 2005, grew up rooting for the Brooklyn Dodgers. As a Little Leaguer, he was a left-handed hitter and his favorite Dodger was outfielder Duke Snider.*

Francis J. "Happy" Felton hosted pregame shows at Ebbets Field. He is pictured here with *(left to right)* Preacher Roe, Duke Snider, Carl Furillo, Gil Hodges and Roy Campanella.

Ralph Branca

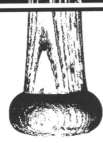

They were linked together for nearly six decades—the batter, the pitcher and the famous home run that occurred in the final playoff game between the New York Giants and the Brooklyn Dodgers on October 3, 1951. Giant Bobby Thomson's three-run blast in the bottom of the ninth inning erased a 4-2 deficit and gave the Giants a 5-4 victory at the Polo Grounds. A Brooklyn Dodger fan, anticipating his team's victory, made a home recording of the ninth inning of the radio broadcast in which the Giants' Russ Hodges excitedly repeats, "The Giants win the pennant! . . . The Giants win the pennant!"

The fan called Hodges later in the week to see if he wanted the recording, a chance opportunity because radio stations in those days rarely archived the games. It became one of the sport's most famous soundtracks, and a painful reminder for Ralph Branca, the Dodger pitcher who by age 21 in 1947 was a 20-game winner. Who could imagine the United States Postal Service in 1998 would issue a stamp commemorating "The Shot Heard 'Round the World" as part of its Celebrate the Century series?

Branca played the role of good sport, posing the following spring of 1952 with his hands around Thomson's neck as the hero smiled. After their respective careers, Branca and Thomson developed a genuine friendship and made the rounds at Old-Timers' days and baseball card shows. Thomson passed away at age 86 in 2010. "Bobby was a really good guy," Branca said. "He was just doing his job and I was doing mine." On the 60th anniversary of the historic home run in 2011, Branca released his autobiography, *A Moment in Time: An American Story of Baseball, Heartbreak and Grace.*

When traded to the Detroit Tigers in 1953, Branca discovered from a former Giant player that New York had rigged an intricate buzzer system at the Polo Grounds to steal signs. Branca kept quiet for nearly 50 years until 2001 when *Wall Street Journal* reporter Josh Prager wrote a detailed account of the sign stealing, which included the use of a vintage World War II spy telescope from a center field clubhouse window of manager Leo Durocher's locked office.

Thomson admitted the Giants stole signs during the 1951 season, in which New York staged a furious comeback after trailing the Dodgers by 13½ games on August 11, but said he wasn't tipped off before Branca's fateful pitch, instead guessing fastball. Branca never asked Thomson the question.

ABOVE Ralph Branca and Bobby Thomson were forever linked after the 1951 National League playoffs and Thomson's "Shot Heard 'Round the World." **OPPOSITE** By age 21, Branca was a 20-game winner.

Ralph Branca

BASE RUNNERS ALLOWED: Excellent, about same as in 1949.

        Newcombe allowed the lowest ON BASE AVERAGE of any one on the staff, his average being 302, an
this was just a trifle higher than his 1949 average of 298 (second best on staff). He did not have an
outstanding record insofar as allowing safehits is concerned, though better than avergge, as he was hi
for a 253 BA (fifth on staff), and the nine inning hit average against him was 8.7. In 1949 he had al
owed fewer safehits as BA against him was 243, and per game hit average was 8.24. However his walk ra
was a bit better than in 1949 so that OBA was only four points worse.

POWER: Very good record, about same as in 1949.

        In 1949 extra-base power against Newcombe had been 46.6%, the best record on the staff, and i
1950 he just about duplicated this performance as power percentage was 46.9%, ranking himsecond among
the staff's regulars (Palica best). He yielded homeruns more frequently than in 1949 allowing a total
of 22 or one every 12.14 innings, and one every 46.32 batters, ranking third best on the staff (behind
Banta, Palica). In 1949 he had allowed one homer every 14.35 innings, every 54 batters. 72.1% of the
hits that he allowed in 1950 were singles, just about the same as his 1949 record (72.2%).

Allan Roth

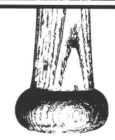

Amember of the Canadian Baseball Hall of Fame, Montreal native Allan Roth (1917-1992) became the first full-time statistician in the Major Leagues when he was hired by the Brooklyn Dodgers in 1947. Along with Dodger Team President Branch Rickey, Roth promoted the idea that on-base percentage was more important than batting average. He also provided special reports for club executives and daily statistical notes for the broadcasters. Roth stayed with the Dodgers through 1964 and was hired by NBC for the network's broadcasts. The Los Angeles chapter of the Society of American Baseball Research (SABR) is named in Roth's honor. In this 1957 interview from a Dodger pregame radio show, Roth described his duties as team statistician:

I see every game, that means both at home and on the road, and I record every pitch. After the game is over I spend about two or three hours entering that data on the statistic sheets for the individual players. During the offseason, I take this terrific amount of detail that I have accumulated and do breakdowns on each of the players on the Dodger club and some of the opposing players. These are complete pitching and batting breakdowns of the players for the front office or the manager. I might have a report on Pee Wee Reese, which would show how Reese hit against right-handed pitchers and left-handers. I also have a breakdown of the Brooklyn batters against the individual pitchers of the National League. So if Bob Rush is pitching for Chicago, the manager knows by looking at a special book how batters like Duke Snider and Carl Furillo have done.

To me, the number of runs batted in doesn't tell the story. If you say Joe Smith knocked in 100 runs last year, that doesn't necessarily mean he's a great clutch hitter. Most baseball men take for granted if a player knocks in 100 runs, he's doing a great job. But it doesn't say how many men he left on base.

Even though I do all these elaborate breakdowns, in the final analysis, the most interesting statistic is the number of games that a team wins. That's what the fan wants to know more than anything else. I think if we can win 95 games or more, that will be the best statistic of all because it likely means the team wins the pennant.

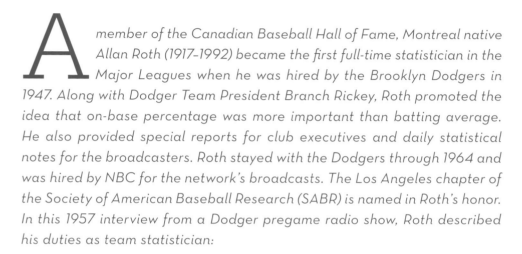

OPPOSITE TOP Allan Roth posed with broadcasters Jerry Doggett, *left*, and Vin Scully, *right*, in the broadcasting booth at the Los Angeles Memorial Coliseum. **OPPOSITE BOTTOM** Roth's scouting report on Don Newcombe, who began his Major League career with the Dodgers in 1949 and became the first player to win the Rookie of the Year, MVP and Cy Young awards in a career. **ABOVE** A 1950 Roth pitching report, "Count on Opposing Hitters when Decisive Pitch Made and Results."

1955 World Series

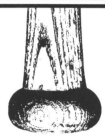

The most significant moment in Brooklyn Dodger history occurred on April 15, 1947, when infielder Jackie Robinson broke baseball's color barrier as the first black player in the 20th century to appear in a Major League game. But the team's most memorable performance took place in Game 7 of the 1955 World Series at Yankee Stadium when Brooklyn starter Johnny Podres hurled a 2–0 masterpiece and the Dodgers captured their first Fall Classic title.

The game was scoreless until the top of the fourth inning when Dodger first baseman Gil Hodges hit a single off Yankee starter Tommy Byrne, who had led the league in winning percentage that year. Hodges later drove in the game's only other run with a sacrifice fly in the sixth inning that scored Pee Wee Reese. In the bottom half of the sixth inning, Sandy Amoros, the Dodgers' speedy reserve outfielder who'd just been inserted into the game, raced to the left field foul line and snagged a fly ball off the bat of Yogi Berra. Amoros turned and fired a relay throw to Reese, who fired a strike to Hodges covering at second base to double up Gil

McDougald. Three innings later, when Elston Howard hit a ground ball to Reese for the final out, Podres, at the tender age of 23, completed his shutout and earned the first World Series MVP Award.

The victory touched off a wild celebration in the borough of Brooklyn, where fans had faithfully followed their beloved "Bums" through previous October heartbreaks. Between 1941 and 1956, the Brooklyn Dodgers would make seven trips to the World Series—each time facing the New York Yankees—including five defeats against the Yankees between 1941 and 1953 and a sixth in 1956.

"That 1955 team will live in Brooklyn Dodger history as long as somebody has a memory," said Carl Erskine, the former pitcher nicknamed "Oisk" who spent his entire career with the Dodgers from 1948 to 1959. "It's hard for people to realize our team agonized for the fans. We would have great teams and go into the World Series with a great record, only to come away empty. I think there was pent-up frustration. When the final out was registered, I knew there was going to be a celebration. But I think winning the World Series was like a spiritual experience; we felt like falling to our knees and thanking the Lord because it took a while."

In a courtyard just outside the main building of the National Baseball Hall of Fame in Cooperstown, New York, sit statues of a pitcher and a catcher that are appropriately placed 60 feet and 6 inches from each another. One reflects the pitching motion of Podres, while the other mirrors the catching stance of Roy Campanella, who was behind the plate during that Game 7 in 1955—a reminder of that game when years of heartache finally gave way to triumph.

ABOVE Third baseman Don Hoak and catcher Roy Campanella greeted Johnny Podres after the left-hander's 2–0 victory in Game 7 of the 1955 World Series. **RIGHT** Newspaper clipping of the box score from Game 7. **OPPOSITE BOTTOM** Team photo of the 1955 World Champion Brooklyn Dodgers.

BROOKLYN (N)

	ab	r	h	po	a
n lf-2b ...	4	0	1	2	0
ss ...	4	1	1	2	6
cf ...	3	0	0	2	0
nella c ...	3	1	1	5	0
rf ...	3	0	0	3	0
1b ...	2	0	1	10	0
b ...	3	0	1	1	1
2b ...	2	0	0	1	2
a ...	1	0	0	0	0
lf ...	0	0	0	2	1
p ...	4	0	0	0	1
s ...	29	2	5	27	11

NEW YORK (A)

	ab	r	h	po	
Rizzuto ss ...	3	0	1	1	
Martin 2b ...	3	0	1	1	
McDougald 3b ...	4	0	3	1	
Berra c ...	4	0	1	4	
Bauer rf ...	4	0	0	1	
Skowron 1b ...	4	0	1	11	
Cerv cf ...	4	0	0	5	
Howard lf ...	4	0	1	2	
Byrne p ...	2	0	0	0	
Grim p ...	0	0	0	0	
b-Mantle ...	1	0	0	0	
Turley p ...	0	0	0	0	
Totals ...	33	0	8	27	1

grounded out for Zimmer in

opped out for Grim in se

LYN (I

ORK (A

ron. R

er, Cam

Left—

Gillian

(Rizz

Reese),

. HO—

yrne 2-

s. L—B

(A), 2I

Schaefer BEER

19 55

WORLD CHAMPION BROOKLYN DODGERS

"Pee Wee" Reese
79-B

"Pee Wee" Reese

Pee Wee Reese

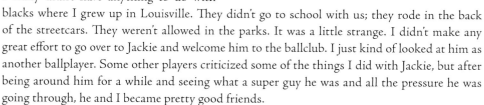

S hortstop Harold "Pee Wee" Reese spent his entire 16-year Major League career with the Dodgers. He appeared in seven World Series and was the Dodgers' team captain during their fabled "Boys of Summer" years in the early 1950s. A Kentucky native, Reese was known for his early support of Brooklyn teammate Jackie Robinson, who broke baseball's color barrier in 1947. When Reese was elected to the Hall of Fame in 1984 by the Veterans Committee, he was asked to recall the first time he heard of Jackie Robinson:

I was stationed in Guam during the war and was coming back from overseas aboard a ship in 1945. We were on the top deck when some kid came up to me and said the Dodgers had signed a black ballplayer. I said, "You've got to be kidding—they didn't sign a black ballplayer." Later, the same fellow came up to me. He must have gotten the news over the wire, and said, "Not only is Jackie black, Pee Wee, but he's also a shortstop." So that kind of concerned me a little bit.

When Jackie first came to the Dodgers, I really didn't have anything to do with blacks where I grew up in Louisville. They didn't go to school with us; they rode in the back of the streetcars. They weren't allowed in the parks. It was a little strange. I didn't make any great effort to go over to Jackie and welcome him to the ballclub. I just kind of looked at him as another ballplayer. Some other players criticized some of the things I did with Jackie, but after being around him for a while and seeing what a super guy he was and all the pressure he was going through, he and I became pretty good friends.

He gives me a lot of credit for helping him, which I'm tickled to death he did because it's nice to be remembered that way. But I think Jackie Robinson did more for me than I ever did for Jackie Robinson. . . .

Jackie had to be the greatest competitor I ever played with. After seeing this fellow play for so many years, and every year we were in a pennant fight, he just showed to me that when the pressure got real tough, Jackie really got going. I saw him make plays during the end of the 1951 season in a series against the Phillies that were unbelievable. He was the guy you really depended on when things got tough.

OPPOSITE 1952 Star-Cal Decal featuring Pee Wee Reese. **ABOVE** On Old-Timers' Day 1984, the Dodgers retired the uniform numbers of Hall of Famers Don Drysdale and Pee Wee Reese.

 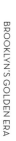

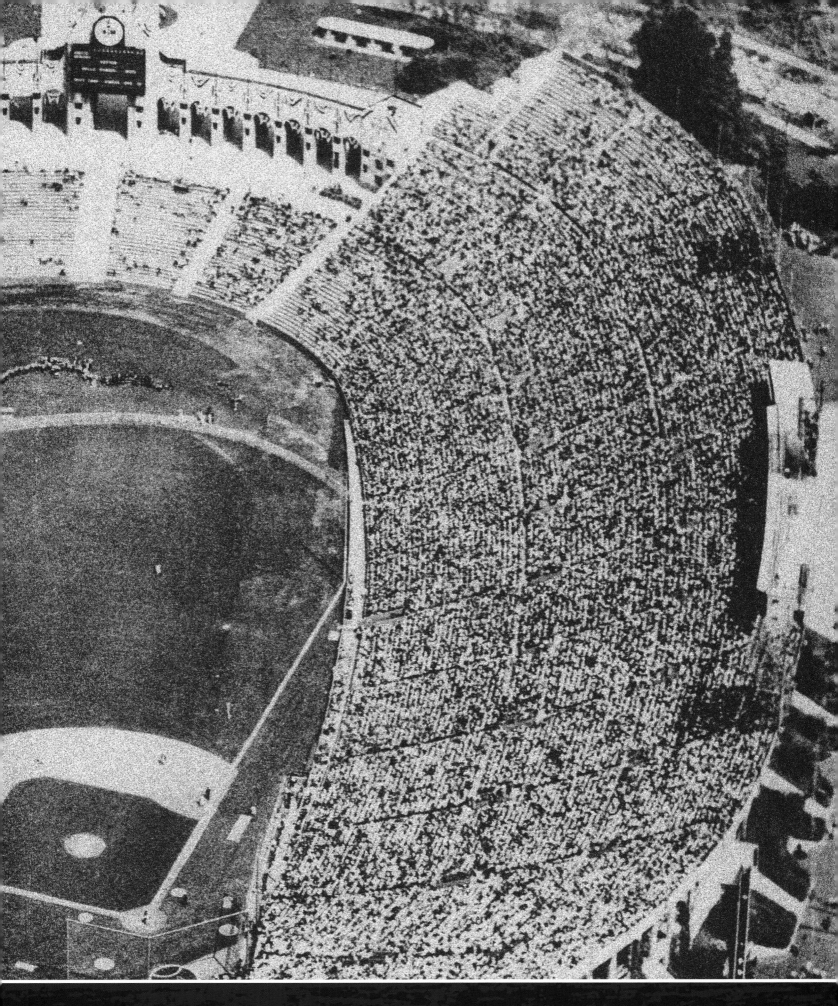

L.A. Coliseum Years
1958–1961

The Coliseum Years

BY WALLY MOON

When I was traded to the Dodgers, I was very aware of the Los Angeles Memorial Coliseum and its baseball layout, having played there with the St. Louis Cardinals in 1958. So there was a little trepidation on my part, along with a little unhappiness that I had been traded. There was the big question: Why would the Dodgers trade for me, a left-handed hitter, to play at the Coliseum? Maybe I was going to be the team's fifth outfielder and a pinch-hitter.

After looking at the Dodgers' lineup and at the Coliseum, my first thought was that I had to play every day on that team. And that means I had to play at the Coliseum as well. I visited my former teammate Stan Musial in St. Louis because I was still upset about the trade. We went out to dinner one night, and Stan said, "Wally, you can hit in any ballpark if you make up your mind to do that and work on it. You just have to adjust to that situation. That little ol' short screen . . . you ought to just pepper it with singles." So I had that thought in my mind when I came to Los Angeles.

Playing at the Coliseum was an exceptionally unique situation. The layout of the ballpark was tremendously deep in right and center fields and then short in left field with that famous screen. When I first came to the Coliseum with the Cardinals in 1958, I thought, "How are they going to play a baseball game in this place?" The second feeling was "You can't see the baseball because of the concrete seats and the peristyle end of the park." In the daytime, there was tremendous glare. The lighting at night was good for football, but you need to see that little baseball pretty well.

We all learned how to play in the Coliseum; I guess you learn to adapt to any situation. But it took some doing. The other thing that was different was the playing field itself: it was not only rough, but also below sea level. So you're down on that field and you're looking up at this cavernous structure. The perspective was so unique. It took some time to stand there at home plate and assess where you were and what you had to do. You finally had to just focus on the pitcher and worry about the baseball coming at you rather than being distracted by all the surroundings.

Early in the 1959 season, Carl Erskine went on the disabled list. He was trying to rework his arm, so he threw hours of batting practice to me, along with a coach named Carroll Beringer. Between those two pitchers, I got a lot of extra work in the Coliseum. I began to pepper the screen with singles and then learned how to loft the ball a little bit. It took some work, but I really and truly enjoyed the challenge.

Clem Labine was a relief pitcher, but he was also good with a fungo bat. Clem would hit fungoes off the left field screen, and I'd play them defensively during practice.

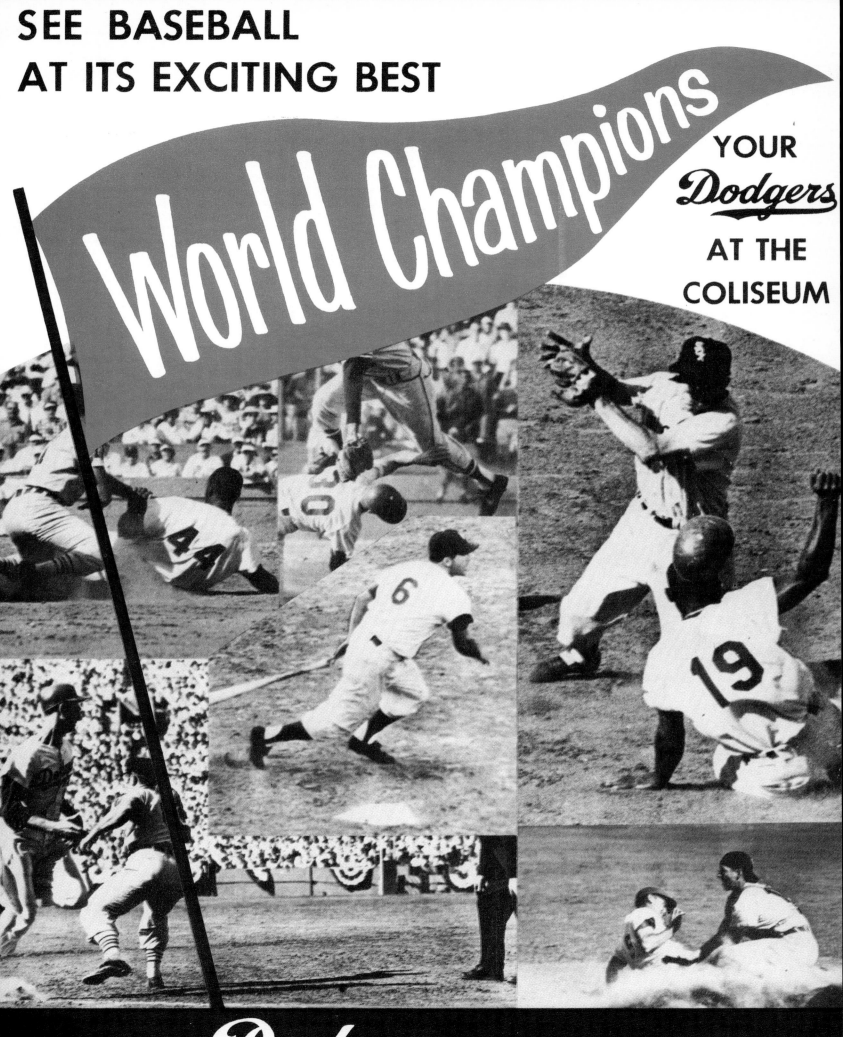

LOS ANGELES Dodgers LINE DRIVES

Vol. 1, No. 1   April, 1958

DODGERS vs GIANTS IN MAJOR LEAGUE DEBUT

DODGERS' DOTS AND DASHES

• • • • • • • • •

Suggested for a visit . . . the Baseball Museum at the Continental Thrift Bank, 5501 Wilshire. Dedication Ceremonies, April 21. Vice-President David Wolper has combed the country for baseball memorabilia, particularly an outstanding collection of Dodger mementos. Mayor Norris Poulson and Governor Goodwin Knight to take part in opening day program.

* * *

KMPC, the Dodgers' station, will offer a 48-inch silver perpetual trophy — the "Golden West Broadcasters' Trophy" — to go to the winner of the annual Los Angeles Dodgers-San Francisco Giants 22-game series. In the event of an 11-11 deadlock in any season, total runs will decide the winner. Gene Autry puts the trophy into competition at Welcome Dodgers Banquet at Biltmore Bowl on eve of Los Angeles opener.

* * *

Sincere thanks of the Dodgers' organization to the Downtown Business Men's Association for their untiring efforts in setting up the Opening Day Parade . . . and a tip of the Dodger cap to all the stores, restaurants and hotels for the tremendous baseball displays for Welcome Dodgers Week (April 14-20).

* * *

HOME SCHEDULE — 1958

April 18, 19, 20	San Francisco
April 22 (N), 23, (N), 24	Chicago
April 25 (N), 26, 27	St. Louis
April 29 (N), 30 (N)	Pittsburgh
May 1 (N), 2 (N), 3	Pittsburgh
May 4 (2), 5 (N), 6 (N), 7	Philadelphia
May 12 (N), 13	San Francisco
June 3 (N), 4 (N), 5	Cincinnati
June 6 (N), 7 (N), 8	Milwaukee
June 10 (N), 11 (N), 12	Philadelphia
June 13 (N), 14 (N), 15	Pittsburgh
July 3 (N-2)	St. Louis
July 5 (N), 6	Chicago
July 9 (N), 10 (N), 11	Milwaukee
July 12, 13 (2), 14	Cincinnati
July 15 (N), 16 (N), 17 (N)	Pittsburgh
July 18 (N), 19 (N), 20	Philadelphia
Aug. 8 (N), 9 (N), 10	San Francisco
Aug. 12 (N), 13 (N), 14	Chicago
Aug. 15 (N-2), 17 (2)	St. Louis
Aug. 19 (N-2), 20 (N), 21 (N), 23	Milwaukee
Aug. 24, 25 (N), 26 (N), 27	Cincinnati

Baseball's Hottest Feud Opens Coliseum Season

Into the world's greatest sports town comes MAJOR LEAGUE BASEBALL at long last! The day all Southern California has been awaiting these many years . . . Friday, April 18:

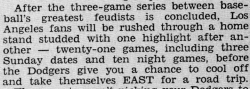

Skipper Alston

Los Angeles Dodgers versus San Francisco Giants.

It is a "Believe It Or Not" cast and setting which five years ago would have been filed in a Hollywood wastepaper basket.

But you can stop pinching yourself. There's this and plenty more to come to your magnificent Los Angeles Memorial Coliseum. And most of it, as they say in the dugout, "right quick."

After the three-game series between baseball's greatest feudists is concluded, Los Angeles fans will be rushed through a home stand studded with one highlight after another — twenty-one games, including three Sunday dates and ten night games, before the Dodgers give you a chance to cool off and take themselves EAST for a road trip.

The experts aren't picking your Dodgers to

ABOVE Cover of the *Line Drives* newsletter highlighting the Dodgers' renewed rivalry with their former New York neighbors. **OPPOSITE** Trumpet-toting fans played the "charge" rally tune at the Coliseum.

Giving up his time and working like that, Clem was so helpful.

Vin Scully first coined that term "Moon Shot" sometime in late May when I hit a long home run. The United States had recently completed an exploration of space, and they were "shooting for the moon." So it all tied together, and Scully is so glib and has that wonderful touch. It was so timely with what was happening—the space outings and the trip to the moon and man going to walk on the moon. It was an exciting time.

Looking back, I did stay in that lineup every day and we did win a championship, so I turned from an unhappy camper to a happy camper. I think that entire Dodger team from 1958 had been disappointed with a seventh-place finish. I remember guys like Duke Snider, Gil Hodges, Pee Wee Reese and Carl Furillo saying, "We're a better ballclub than that." We had a few team meetings in the spring. As I got to know the players, I began to see the cohesiveness of the group, and I felt good about that, even though it still was only the spring. I think

everyone from Walter Alston and the coaching staff to Buzzie Bavasi started to pump themselves up early in the spring and said, "Let's have a better year." I could see the Dodgers had great pitching with Don Drysdale, Sandy Koufax, Johnny Podres and Ed Roebuck. I felt good about playing for Alston. He was smooth and a quiet guy who just expected you to do your best. He and I had some really good conversations in Spring Training.

The 1959 season was a patchwork effort of a lot of good players. No great big stars. Everybody made a contribution. We won a lot of close games and worked hard every day to be a good ballclub. That feeling kept growing. I think it was a championship year from the heart rather from the total talent. I felt very confident about our pennant chances. It was a spectacular finish with a playoff against the Milwaukee Braves and then a tremendous World Series against the Chicago White Sox.

As for the big crowds at the Coliseum, I don't have the words to describe the feeling of 92,000 people rooting for a player or a team. The swell of applause was enormous

for good plays or good pitching. Here we were in the World Series, and all those people are rooting for us. How could it be any better than that?

By 1961, the Dodgers were getting ready to move from the Coliseum into their new ballpark for the 1962 season. There was some nostalgia as we were leaving because we had accomplished something unique by playing at the Coliseum. But there was great excitement about Chavez Ravine and Dodger Stadium coming out of the ground. All of us players were playing at the Coliseum and going over to see what was happening at Chavez Ravine. I was so interested in the construction and the location of the ballpark and the possibilities it would provide to our Dodger team. I personally enjoyed the Coliseum more than any other player did, but I was also anxious to leave the Coliseum, so I had the best of both worlds.

*Outfielder **Wally Moon** is the Dodger player most associated with the Los Angeles Memorial Coliseum, where a 42-foot screen was erected in left field to prevent easy home runs over its unusually close left field fence. The left field fence was a mere 251 feet from home plate, which led to new stadiums requiring a minimum of 325 feet down the foul lines.*

1959
WORLD SERIES
LOS ANGELES MEMORIAL COLISEUM
LOS ANGELES, CALIFORNIA

FIELD

NOT GOOD ON FIELD DURING GAME
NOT GOOD FOR ADMISSION

MUST BE DISPLAYED
WHEN ON FIELD
SUBJECT TO CONDITIONS
ON BACK

NO 51

Los Angeles
Dodgers

1958 SCHEDULE
HOME

18, 19, 20	San Francisco
22(N), 23(N), 24	Chicago
25(N), 26, 27	St. Louis
29(N), 30(N)	Pittsburgh
1(N), 2(N), 3	Pittsburgh
4(2), 5(N), 6(N), 7	Philadelphia
12(N), 13	San Francisco
3(N), 4(N), 5	Cincinnati
6(N), 7(N), 8	Milwaukee
10(N), 11(N), 12	Philadelphia
13(N), 14(N), 15	Pittsburgh
3(N-2)	St. Louis
5(N), 6	Chicago
9(N), 10(N), 11	Milwaukee
12, 13(2), 14	Cincinnati
15(N), 16(N), 17(N)	Pittsburgh
18(N), 19(N), 20	Philadelphia
ugust 8(N), 9(N), 10	San Francisco
ugust 12(N), 13(N), 14	Chicago
ugust 15(N-2), 17(2)	St. Louis
ugust 19(N-2), 20(N), 21(N), 23	Milwaukee
ugust 24, 25(N), 26(N), 27	Cincinnati
eptember 2(N), 3(N), 4	San Francisco
eptember 23(N), 24(N)	St. Louis
eptember 26(N-2), 27	Chicago

1958 SCHEDULE
AWAY

April 15, 16(N), 17	San Francisco
May 9(N), 10, 11	San Francisco
May 14, 15	Chicago
May 16(N), 17, 18(2)	St. Louis
May 20(N), 21	Milwaukee
May 22(N), 23(N), 24	Cincinnati
May 25, 26(N)	Philadelphia
May 27(N), 28(N)	Pittsburgh
May 30(2), 31	Chicago
June 1	Chicago
June 17(N), 18(N), 19(N)	Philadelphia
June 20(N), 21, 22(2)	Pittsburgh
June 23(N), 24(N), 25(N)	Cincinnati
June 26(N), 27(N), 28, 29	Milwaukee
June 30(N)	St. Louis
July 1(N)	St. Louis
July 22(N), 23(N), 24	Pittsburgh
July 25(N), 26(N), 27	Philadelphia
July 29(N), 30(N), 31	Milwaukee
August 1(N), 2, 3(2)	Cincinnati
August 4(N), 5	St. Louis
August 6, 7	Chicago
August 29(N), 30, 31	San Francisco
September 1(A.M. & P.M.)	San Francisco
September 5(N), 6(N), 7	St. Louis
September 9(N), 10(N), 11(N)	Philadelphia
September 12(N), 13	Pittsburgh
September 14, 15	Milwaukee
September 16(N)	Cincinnati
September 19, 20, 21	Chicago

(N) Nights   (N-2) Twi-night Doubleheaders   (2) Doubleheaders

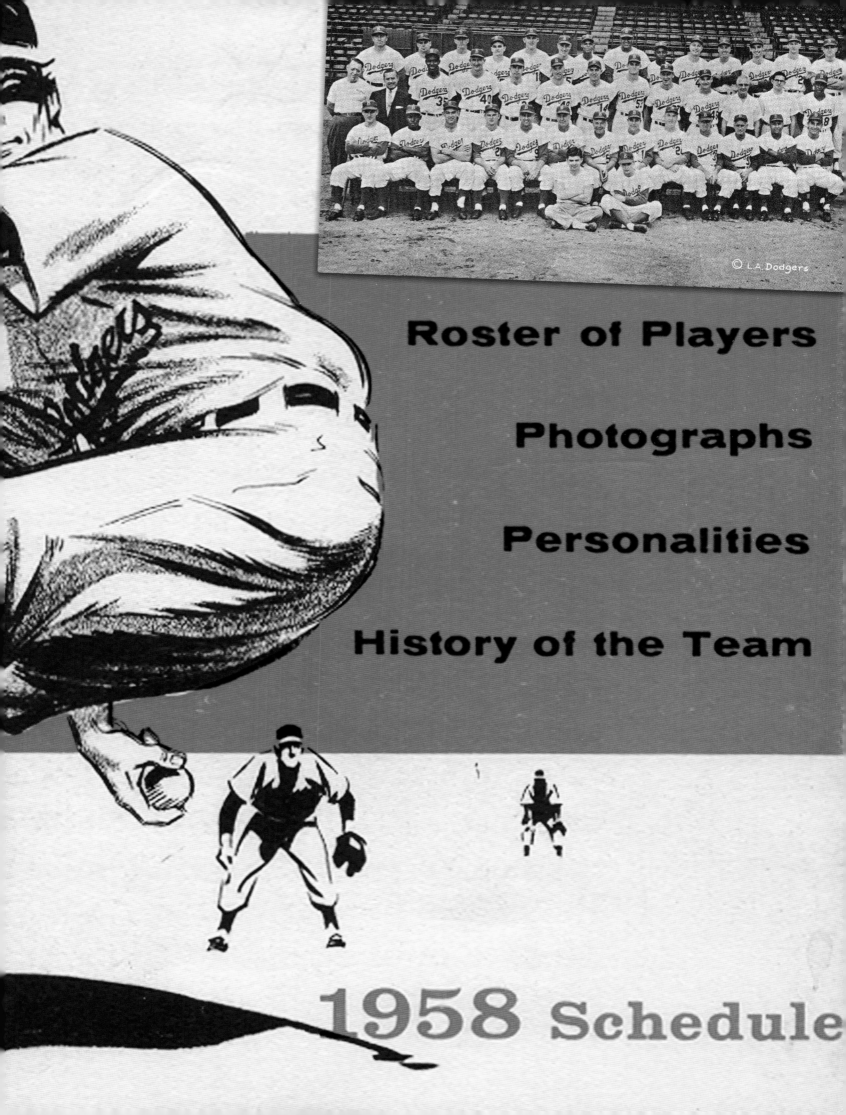

Roster of Players

Photographs

Personalities

History of the Team

© L.A. Dodgers

1958 Schedule

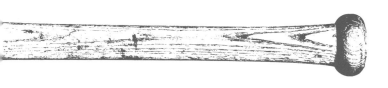

Rosalind Wyman

A s a newly elected member of the Los Angeles City Council in 1953, Rosalind "Roz" Wyman set her sights high when she decided Major League Baseball should be part of the city's landscape. Southern California had two teams in the Pacific Coast League—the Hollywood Stars and Los Angeles Angels—but Wyman and other city officials reasoned that Los Angeles' climate and population would be ideal for a franchise wanting to relocate. No Major League team had switched cities for 50 years until the National League Braves moved from Boston to Milwaukee during Spring Training in 1953.

In May 1955, Los Angeles voters rejected a $4.5 million bond proposal to build a baseball stadium, which meant public funding wasn't a bargaining chip for Wyman when she wrote a letter on September 1 to Dodger Owner Walter O'Malley. Wyman hoped for a meeting to gauge O'Malley's interest in moving his Brooklyn franchise, but the Dodgers were in the midst of a pennant race and O'Malley still held out hope he could work with New York officials for a new ballpark to replace the aging Ebbets Field.

Wyman, along with Los Angeles Mayor Norris Poulson and County Supervisor Kenneth Hahn, kept lobbying, and their efforts finally paid off when a perfect storm of events gave the Dodgers a reason to look elsewhere. The Dodgers were getting nowhere with New York officials, and Horace Stoneham of the rival New York Giants was considering moving his team to Minneapolis.

Early in 1957, O'Malley secured the Southern California territorial rights from Phil Wrigley of the Chicago Cubs by acquiring the PCL Angels franchise. Mayor Poulson sent Harold "Chad" McClellan to New York as the official negotiator on behalf of Los Angeles. The National League, meanwhile, gave its approval if the Dodgers and Giants both wanted to relocate after the season.

On September 17, 1957, the Los Angeles City Council passed a resolution by an 11–3 vote to offer a deal to the Dodgers to privately finance and construct a 50,000-seat stadium on the Chavez Ravine property, which was the site of a discontinued public housing project from the early 1950s.

On October 7, a phone call featuring intrigue on both sides set the stage for the dramatic final vote by the City Council on whether to formally offer the deal or not. O'Malley called Poulson, who handed the phone to Wyman. She was confident the resolution would pass but wary of celebrating too early. And even if approved, Wyman couldn't be sure of O'Malley's intentions. "He never actually said he was coming," Wyman recalled years later. Fortunately, none of Wyman's colleagues asked if O'Malley was wavering on his decision. The City Council adopted the ordinance by a 10–4 margin.

The next day, the Dodgers issued a press release to announce they were moving. "In view of the action of the Los Angeles City Council yesterday and in accordance with the resolution of the National League made October first, the stockholders and directors of the Brooklyn Baseball Club have today met and unanimously agreed that the necessary steps be taken to draft the Los Angeles territory."

OPPOSITE Rosalind Wyman greeted Walter O'Malley along with Los Angeles city officials Gordon Hahn, *left*, and Kenneth Hahn, *right*.
ABOVE In 2011 Wyman posed with a 1957 *Los Angeles Times*, touting the Dodgers' decision to move from Brooklyn.

1958 Opening Day

The dawn of a new era meant a final sleepless night for an old warhorse. When Carl Erskine woke up on the morning of April 18, 1958, he realized he was about to pitch the final significant game of a distinguished Major League career. Battling arm problems at age 31, Erskine already had pitched in five World Series and authored two no-hitters during his prime with the Brooklyn Dodgers.

The Dodgers and the Giants left New York and relocated to the West Coast during the previous winter, settling in Los Angeles and San Francisco, respectively. Opening Day in Los Angeles represented a kaleidoscope of baseball history, local tradition, civic pride and pregame anticipation. Although the Pacific Coast League—including the local Hollywood Stars and Los Angeles Angels—was a fixture for more than four decades in major California communities, the high-profile "Boys of Summer" Dodgers meant national baseball exposure for a city long associated with the major football tenants at the Los Angeles Memorial Coliseum: the USC Trojans, the UCLA Bruins and the Los Angeles Rams.

With Erskine's first pitch to Giant rookie Jim Davenport at 1:45 that sunny Friday afternoon, the landscape of the sporting scene in Los Angeles was forever changed. "That first pitch in Los Angeles . . . I wanted it to be a strike," Erskine said. "I thought about it all night."

The Dodgers began the day with a special ceremony on the Spring Street steps of City Hall at 10:30 a.m. As the uniformed players sat down, señoritas from Olvera Street took off their caps and cracked their heads with *cascarones*— confetti-filled eggs—for good luck. Dodger President Walter O'Malley presented an autographed home plate to Los Angeles Mayor Norris Poulson. After the speeches, the Dodgers paraded down Broadway in a motorcade of open cars, their names bannered on the side.

A crowd of 78,762 watched Erskine and the Dodgers escape with a 6–5 victory. Trailing 6–4 in the ninth inning, the Giants staged a rally when Davenport chased Erskine with a leadoff double and Willie Kirkland tripled off reliever Clem Labine. But Davenport stumbled while rounding third, and Los Angeles rookie Dick Gray noticed Davenport failed to touch the base en route to scoring. The Dodgers appealed the play, and Davenport was called out. Willie Mays hit an RBI single, but Labine retired Daryl Spencer and Orlando Cepeda to end the game.

The 1958 Dodgers finished in seventh place with a 71-83 record. At the box office, more than 1.8 million fans watched the new team at the Coliseum. "That Opening Day in 1958 made the whole year a success," said former Dodger Executive Vice President Buzzie Bavasi, who passed away at age 93 in 2008. "Back east, we took everything for granted because baseball was the only game in town. Brooklyn didn't have a professional football or basketball team. Here in Los Angeles, we thought we'd have to battle for the support of the fans. Instead, it came naturally."

ABOVE Joe E. Brown with San Francisco coach Herman Franks (subbing for ailing manager Bill Rigney) and Dodger manager Walter Alston. **RIGHT** Brown's pregame script from the 1958 Opening Day ceremonies.

members of the official Dodger family and two of

baseball's most dedicated people...Mr. and Mrs. James A. Mulvey.

* * *

"And now, let's bring some of our dignitaries out here on the

field...The man who led the fight to bring baseball to the

West Coast...Your Los Angeles Mayor Norris Poulson..

(((MAYOR POULSON GOES BEHIND THE PITCHING MOUND)))

"A man who was equally zealous in his efforts to corral the Giants..

from San Francisco, Mayor George Christopher..

((((MAYOR CHRISTOPHER JOINS POULSON)))

"And here is Mr. Baseball, folks, the Commissioner of Baseball...

Ford C. Frick.. ((((FRICK JOINS MAYORS))))

"And President of the National League who helped steer the ex-

pansion of the game to the Pacific Coast...Warren C. Giles..

(((GILES JOINS GROUP))))

"I'm now going to ask the managers

give me their starting line-ups fo

on out here... From San Francisco..

Rigney...

* * *

And, folks, how about a real hand fo

Angeles Dodgers... Manager Walt Alst

* * *

"Bill, we wish you all sorts of luck

the Dodgers, but I hope you won't min

flowers...But here, to offer an Openir

OUR Skipper are Mr. W. J. Vander-Brugg

of the Southern California Florists As

TIME SCHEDULE AND SCRIPT

LOS ANGELES DODGERS' HOME OPENER

APRIL 18 VS SAN FRANCISCO GIANTS   1958

* * *

TIME SCHEDULE

TICKETS ON SALE . . . . .9:30 A.M. (Peristyle E

GATES OPEN .11:00 A.M.

GIANTS' BATTING PRACTICE . . . . .11:15 TO 12:00

JOHNNY BOUDREAU'S BAND CONCERT . . . . .12:00 - NOON

DODGERS' BATTING PRACTICE . . . . .12:00 TO 12:45 P.M.

DODGERS' INFIELD PRACTICE . . . . .12:45 TO 1:00 P.M.

GIANTS' INFIELD PRACTICE . . . . .1:00 TO 1:15 P.M.

FIELD IS CLEARED OF ALL BUT PRE-GAME . . . . .1:15 P.M.
PARTICIPANTS AND PHOTOGRAPHERS

GROUNDSKEEPERS . . . . .1:15 TO 1:30 P.M.

PRE-GAME CEREMONIES . . . . .1:30 TO 1:45 P.M.

"PLAY BALL" .1:45 P.M.

* * * *

PRE-GAME SCRIPT

((11:59 - JUST BEFORE DODGERS' BATTING PRACTICE))

RAMSEY: . . . ." Attention Please, Ladies and Gentlemen . . . . . now, takin

their first batting practice in their new home, YOUR Los

Angeles Dodgers...."

((12:00))

for your listening entertainment, an old

DUKE SNIDER NIGHT

AUGUST 26, 1960

LOS ANGELES COLISEUM

SOUVENIR BOOK

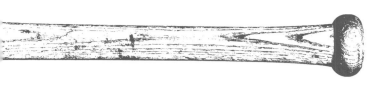

Duke Snider

W hen the Dodgers moved to the West Coast in 1958, the players didn't see the actual baseball field tucked within the cavernous Los Angeles Memorial Coliseum until the first home game on April 18. Willie Mays of the San Francisco Giants played the role of unwanted tour guide when he intercepted center fielder Duke Snider as he walked from the dressing room toward the field. "Look where that right field fence is, Duke," Mays shouted. "They sure fixed you up good. You couldn't reach it with a cannon. You're done, man!"

The mighty "Duke of Flatbush," Brooklyn's career home run leader with 316 from 1947 to 1957 and five consecutive seasons of 40 or more home runs, was stunned. It wasn't the homecoming he expected as a graduate of nearby Compton High School and one of the few Dodgers with Southern California roots. The Coliseum's makeshift baseball field within a football and track venue meant a unique layout. Left field was 251 feet from home plate; left center, 400 feet; center, 425 feet; right center, 440 feet; right field, 300 feet.

Snider hit just 15 home runs in 1958 (six at the Coliseum), and the Dodgers finished in seventh place. At the crossroads of his career at age 31, the stubborn Snider refused to change his swing and remained a pull hitter. Snider got back on track with 23 home runs in 1959 (13 at home) to help the Dodgers reach the World Series. A knee injury limited Snider's playing time in the 1959 World Series against the Chicago White Sox, but he managed to hit a home run in the team's title-clinching 9–3 victory in Game 6 at Chicago's Comiskey Park. It was the 11th career World Series home run for Snider, which at the time placed him in a tie for second with the Yankees' Mickey Mantle behind Babe Ruth's all-time record of 15 postseason home runs.

Snider's most memorable moment at the Coliseum didn't involve his bat. During batting practice in June 1958, Snider and infielder Don Zimmer were discussing the size of their new ballpark when Zimmer came up with a challenge. Could the strong-armed Snider throw a ball out of the park, aiming from the outfield toward the top of the Coliseum? Snider thought he could, so Zimmer collected $400 worth of bets from teammates. Snider came close on three tries, but he injured his elbow on the final attempt and was fined $200 by Executive Vice President Buzzie Bavasi.

Snider wasn't seriously hurt, so Zimmer held the money in escrow until the final game of the season. Snider threw the ball out of the ballpark on his first try and collected his $200 share. During the winter, Bavasi asked Snider if he had learned his lesson. Snider said, "I don't think I'll ever learn my lesson, Buzzie, but the arm feels much better." Bavasi refunded the $200.

ABOVE When Duke Snider's uniform No. 4 was retired in 1980 at Dodger Stadium, he entered the ballpark through the center field fence along with fellow Hall of Famers Willie Mays (No. 24) and Joe DiMaggio (No. 5).

LOS ANGELES *Do*

IN FULL NATURAL COLOR

LOS ANGELES
MEMORIAL
COLISEUM

dgers

STAMP

LAD

WORLD CHAMPIONS

LOS ANGELES

Dodgers

SOUVENIR **1960** YEAR BOOK   50¢

Jim Gilliam

Nine of the 10 retired numbers in Dodger history belong to Hall of Fame players and managers. The exception is Jim Gilliam, the National League's Rookie of the Year in 1953 who remained with the Dodger organization until his death at age 49 prior to the 1978 World Series. Although lacking the gaudy stats that often lead to Cooperstown enshrinement, this two-time All-Star brought value to the team over a career that saw him play a key role in four World Series titles.

Along with manager Walter Alston, the Tennessee native was the bridge between Brooklyn's only World Championship in 1955 and the first three titles on the West Coast in 1959, 1963 and 1965. Gilliam's ability to play three positions—second base, third base and left field—gave Alston flexibility with his starting lineup. At the plate, Gilliam was a switch-hitter who rarely struck out, making him a handy accomplice to Maury Wills' base-stealing exhibitions in the 1960s.

Gilliam began his professional career with the Baltimore Elite Giants of the Negro Leagues. The Dodgers acquired Gilliam and pitcher Joe Black from Baltimore following the 1950 season. Gilliam spent the 1951 and 1952 seasons at Triple-A Montreal of the International League, waiting for his chance in Brooklyn. After Gilliam's strong Spring Training performance in

1953, Jackie Robinson agreed to switch from second base to third base. Gilliam accepted the challenge and helped the Dodgers win a club-record 105 games en route to the pennant. Gilliam garnered top rookie honors by batting .271 with 125 runs, 100 walks and 21 stolen bases. His 21 triples led the league and were the most by a Dodger since Hi Myers had 22 triples in 1920.

During the 1959 championship season in Los Angeles, Gilliam led the league in walks (96) and singles (131). He stole 23 bases, leading the team in that category for the sixth consecutive season, and grounded into only three double plays. In 1960, Wills began batting leadoff, and Gilliam protected him in the No. 2 slot by taking pitches and often letting himself fall behind two strikes in the count.

Throughout his tenure as a player, Gilliam was the subject of trade rumors because of the seemingly endless list of prospects ready to take his job: Charlie Neal, Don Zimmer, Dick Gray, John Werhas, Jim Baxes, Ken McMullen and Nate Oliver. Gilliam retired as a player following the 1964 season and joined Alston's coaching staff. But a slow start in 1965 by third baseman John Kennedy prompted Executive Vice President Buzzie Bavasi to activate Gilliam, who at age 36 batted .280 in 111 games.

Gilliam's most famous moment occurred in the decisive Game 7 of the 1965 World Series at Minnesota. Trailing 2–0 in the fifth inning, the Twins had Dodger ace Sandy Koufax, pitching on two days' rest, on the ropes with one out and two runners on base. Zoilo Versalles pulled a sharp grounder over the third base bag. Gilliam made a lunging stab, changed directions and raced to the bag to force Frank Quilici at third. Koufax settled down and completed the shutout. The Baseball Hall of Fame called and requested Gilliam's glove.

ABOVE The Dodgers retired Jim Gilliam's uniform No. 19 prior to the 1978 World Series.

JIM GILLIAM

L.A. Dodgers official

47. Clip-on glasses....... .... 1.00

48. Binoculars...................... 1.50

49. Dodger colored picture pennant.......... 1.50

50. Dodger picture badges. C... Snider, W. Davis, Howar... Drysdale, Moon. ...... Set of 5

51. All National League team pennants - ea. $1.00 .... Set of 8...... 7.00

52. Dodger pennant.....................

Kids' pullover sweatshirt - Sizes 4 - 16 .... 3.00

55. Dodger bath towel..............

Dodger kids' jacket - Sizes 4-20

.... 1.50

58. Set of 10 3½" x 5½" Dodger player pictures - full color. ....

Dodger lighters.........
Dodger ash tray........

...otorola Transistor Radio.. 20.00

MOTOROLA

62. Dodgers' Way to Play Baseball 1.50

63. Dodger baby bib apron 1.00

64. Dodger Pen and Post Card ....

BRAVES CARDINALS CUBS Phillies GIANTS REDS Dodgers PIRATES

LOS ANGELES

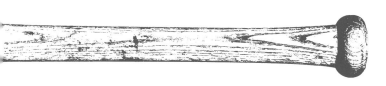

Danny Goodman

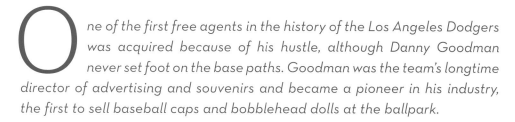

O ne of the first free agents in the history of the Los Angeles Dodgers was acquired because of his hustle, although Danny Goodman never set foot on the base paths. Goodman was the team's longtime director of advertising and souvenirs and became a pioneer in his industry, the first to sell baseball caps and bobblehead dolls at the ballpark.

The Milwaukee native dropped out of high school at age 15 and began a career in sales to help support his widowed mother. Goodman peddled beer at local minor league games and sold candy in nightclubs. He learned two basic lessons about sports fans: "People eat their damn heads off at ballgames," and "They like to have something to show they were there."

From 1933 to 1937, Goodman was concessions manager of the Newark Bears, the New York Yankees' top minor league affiliate. When Goodman opened the first novelty stand of any ballpark in the country, Newark Team President George Weiss didn't believe fans would be interested. "Eventually, there will be a lot of money made off novelties," Goodman predicted.

When he moved to California in 1938, Goodman quickly established himself with the Southern California sports and entertainment communities. As concessions manager and advertising director of the Hollywood Stars, Goodman worked for the Pacific Coast League franchise owned by Robert Cobb, who also operated the famous Brown Derby restaurant. In 1946, Goodman suggested to Cobb that the grounds crew should "tidy up" the infield between the fourth and fifth innings. The idea was to delay the action to buy time for the concessionaires.

Goodman also became entertainment director of the Friars Club in Beverly Hills, putting on testimonial dinners and luncheons for more than 150 sports and show business personalities. A testimonial dinner in 1955 honoring Goodman featured such stars as Ronald Reagan, Jack Benny, George Burns, Phil Silvers, Dean Martin, Leo Durocher, Charlie Dressen, Casey Stengel, Ty Cobb, Fred Haney, Tom Harmon, Buddy Hackett and others.

During his prime with the Dodgers, Goodman carried more than 150 different items, the largest assortment in sports, and 40 percent of his sales were mail orders. Goodman's marketing imagination was balanced by his sense of humor, and he knew that the next "sure thing" could flop or that a pennant-race swoon could leave piles of obsolete playoff merchandise.

With the Dodgers playing at the 90,000-seat Los Angeles Memorial Coliseum, Goodman purchased 75,000 plastic bugles that had three keys and blew "Charge." Goodman also gambled that fans attending the three afternoon games of the 1959 World Series would want protection from the sun. He sold 80,000 straw hats.

"The time when the Dodgers played at the Coliseum was the first time novelties were sold in large promotion and production in any sports stadium or arena," Goodman said in 1976. "Novelty manufacturers sprung up like mushrooms all over the country, and that really was the beginning of large-scale novelty promotions at any sports stadium."

ABOVE Goodman was a pioneer in his industry and was the Dodgers' director of advertising and souvenirs from 1958 to 1984.

Campy Night

When the Dodgers celebrated the 37th birthday of shortstop Pee Wee Reese in 1955, the plan was to turn Brooklyn's Ebbets Field into a giant birthday cake by dimming the stadium lights and asking fans to bring anything they could light—candles, matches, cigars, cigarettes. Reese may have worn uniform No. 1, but he didn't want to be the only figure at home plate when the crowd sang "Happy Birthday." A nervous Reese asked teammate Roy Campanella to stand alongside him during the festivities.

Four years later, the Dodgers staged a similar ceremony, but under much different circumstances. The franchise had moved from Brooklyn to Los Angeles after the 1957 season, and Campanella, a Dodger since 1948 and a three-time National League MVP, traveled to Southern California during the winter to attend baseball banquets and other events promoting the Dodgers' new home. The catcher signed his 1958 contract, but weeks before Spring Training, he was involved in an auto accident in New York while driving from his liquor store in Harlem to

his home in Glen Cove. His rented car skidded on an icy patch in the road and struck a telephone pole. Campanella was paralyzed from the shoulders down.

The Dodgers and the New York Yankees staged a benefit game on the Thursday evening of May 7, 1959, to help defray Campanella's medical bills. The Dodgers, who played an afternoon game at San Francisco that day, and the Yankees, traveling from Kansas City, made a special trip to the Los Angeles Memorial Coliseum for the exhibition game, which drew a record crowd of 93,103.

In the fifth inning, the game was stopped and the stadium lights were dimmed. On the radio, broadcaster Vin Scully described the scene when the crowd struck matches on the cue of public address announcer John Ramsey: "A sea of lights at the Coliseum . . . perhaps the most beautiful and dramatic moment in the history of sports. Let there be a prayer for every light, and wherever you are, maybe you in silent tribute to Campanella can also say a prayer for his well-being. . . . Roy Campanella, for thousands of times, made a trip to the mound to help somebody out—a tired pitcher, a disgusted youngster, a boy who perhaps had his heart broken in the game of baseball. And tonight, on his last trip to the mound, the city of Los Angeles says hello to him."

In the darkened ballpark, Reese, now a Dodger coach, pushed Campanella's wheelchair to the pitcher's mound. Campanella turned to Reese and said, "Now you have to stand by me."

ABOVE Former teammate Pee Wee Reese pushed Roy Campanella's wheelchair during ceremonies honoring the Hall of Fame catcher. **OPPOSITE** Souvenir scorecard from Roy Campanella Night featured a portrait by artist Nicholas Volpe.

LOS ANGELES

Dodgers

"CAMPY"   SOUVENIR ISSUE

LOS ANGELES COLISEUM   1959   OFFICIAL DODGER SCORE CARD 20¢

WORLD 1959 SERIES

COMISKEY PARK

AMERICAN LEAGUE vs.
NATIONAL LEAGUE

WHITE SOX

LOWER GAME RAIN CHECK
GRAND 6 RETAIN THIS CHECK
STAND NOT GOOD IF DETACHED
$7.20
(TAX INCLUDED) PLAYED UNDER THE
SUPERVISION OF
FORD C. FRICK
COMMISSIONER OF BASEBALL

ENTER GATE 5
35th ST. EAST

Lower Grandstand $7.20

SEC. ROW SEAT
12 20 18

DO NOT DETACH THIS
COUPON FROM RAIN CHECK

LOS ANGELES, CALIF.
OFFICIAL SOUVENIR PROGRAM

50¢

1959 Championship

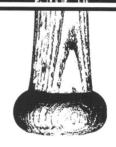

I n 1959, the Dodgers became the first franchise in Major League history to win a World Series following a seventh-place finish the previous season. The Los Angeles Dodgers and the Milwaukee Braves were tied at 86-68 at the end of the regular season. After losing the two previous NL playoffs in 1946 (St. Louis Cardinals) and 1951 (New York Giants), the Dodgers won the first two games of the best-of-three playoff against the Braves. In the World Series, the Dodgers defeated the Chicago White Sox in six games. Rookie reliever Larry Sherry, who posted two victories and two saves against Chicago, earned World Series MVP honors. During the 1959 regular season, Sherry was 7-2 with a 2.19 ERA in 23 games for Los Angeles after a midseason promotion from the team's Triple-A St. Paul affiliate. In this excerpt from a 2007 interview with team historian Mark Langill, former Dodger Executive Vice President Buzzie Bavasi looked back on the first title in Los Angeles history:

Of all the Dodger clubs I had, the 1959 club was one of the weakest because we had a second baseman playing the outfield (Jim Gilliam), a first baseman playing right field (Ron Fairly) and Norm Larker and others playing all over the place. We had no set positions.

I give credit to John Corriden for the 1959 World Series, believe it or not. John was a scout around 80 years old, living in Indianapolis. And I believe in old scouts. I called him during the season and said, "John, we need a relief pitcher. Find one for me." He scouted the minor leagues and finally called, saying, "I found one for you. Larry Sherry." I said, "C'mon, John. He's been with us for two years and he can't pitch." John said, "What are you paying me for, Buzzie? You want information, and I'm giving it to you. If you don't bring him up to the Dodgers, then I quit, so help me."

So we brought up Larry to the Dodgers, and the rest is history. Carl Erskine retired, and Larry, along with Roger Craig, took his place. We finished the regular season tied with the Braves for first place. During the first playoff game against Milwaukee, Larry was brought out of the bullpen in the second inning while John Corriden was home in Indianapolis, seated in front of his television set. As Larry was coming into the game, [Corriden] asked his wife, "Could you bring me a lollipop?" That was John's phrase for a beer. She said, "Sure." When she came back to give John the beer, he was dead in his chair. He never saw Larry pitch that first playoff game. Larry wound up pitching 7⅔ innings in relief of Danny McDevitt that afternoon.

I think Larry did a helluva job, but I think he was doing an ever better job because of John Corriden. What can I say about Larry's performance against the White Sox? All I can do is praise him. Everybody knows Larry Sherry won the World Series for us.

OPPOSITE BOTTOM Charlie Neal, *left,* with Chuck Essegian. **ABOVE** Jerry Doggett interviewed *(left to right)* Wally Moon, Sandy Koufax and John Roseboro. **ABOVE RIGHT** Vin Scully and Series MVP Larry Sherry.

107

"You must come out to see

"this beautiful ball park"

The 1960s

Pitching, Speed and Defense

BY TOMMY DAVIS

When Dodger Stadium opened in 1962, I thought it was an outstanding facility and such a beautiful place. I felt fortunate to be on the first Dodger team that played there. As a young player, I thought if I did well, I could stay for a while. When we played at the Coliseum, I didn't like the line drives that hit the screen in left field. I must've lost six or seven home runs. Instead of going into a home run trot, I had to hustle to first base, because the ball would drop straight down after hitting the screen and the left fielder could make a play at first base—at least, that's how close it seemed with the fence just 250 feet from home plate. Dodger Stadium was measured equally in the outfield, so it was suited for me, because I sprayed the ball to all fields, so the defense couldn't play me a certain way.

The 1962 season was my third year in the Majors, and I had a chance to play more. I didn't expect to get 230 hits and have 153 RBI in the same year, but everything seemed to fall into place. The more you play, the more you learn about yourself as a ballplayer. I never wanted to be Jackie Robinson, who was my idol as a kid, but I did want to be like him in terms of always making contact. I wanted to hit line drives, and I didn't feel like I needed to hit a lot of home runs to help the team. I had a lot of speed in those days, and I was also lucky. I had a chance to drive in a lot of runs because I always had speedsters like Maury Wills, Jim Gilliam and Willie Davis on base ahead of me.

I also benefited tremendously from having Frank Howard hit behind me in the lineup. A lot of opposing pitchers didn't want to face Howard, because he hit balls so hard, they could take a man's head off. With Howard in the lineup, I always got a couple of good pitches I could drive somewhere. And in my opinion, Jim Gilliam was the best No. 2 hitter in baseball and should be in the Hall of Fame. Gilliam could do so many things, play so many positions and do whatever needed to be done to win a close ballgame.

It was very exciting in 1962 when the Dodgers were winning games and it looked like we were going to the

"Mule Trains" . . . new comforts for the fans. The Dodgers will offer special cars to bring patrons from the more distant areas of the parking facilities, right to the proper section.

Your *Dodger* home of tomorrow

Four-tier stands . . . Two-thirds of the seats will be between the baselines and approximately ninety-five percent within the foul lines. Thanks to pre-cast concrete construction of the Stadium and roof, there will not be a single column obstructing the vision of the fans. All seats will afford not only a clear view of the game but also a sweeping sky-high panorama of the Los Angeles area. At night games it will be an unmatched spectacle—a light-flooded ball field with the beautiful jeweled City of Los Angeles as a backdrop.

Panorama . . . artist's conception of the new Stadium as it will be set high in the rugged Chavez Ravine terrain. A perimeter road system will feed into terraced parking areas so that all fans will walk horizontally to the entrances leading to their sections. Colored tickets, matching the horticultural display of each terrace and the corresponding section of the stands will acquaint the fans with the most convenient place to park. There will be room for more than 17,000 cars and busses.

For those fans who wish to use bus transportation there will be special loading zones and express lanes.

Cross section . . . a profile view of stands. Note that aisles feed each elevation from the top. Fans will walk an average of ten feet (down) to seats. It is a ball park built FOR the fans —the Dodgers' and Baseball's $12,000,000 contribution to modern, clean, comfortable and convenient facilities that the best sports-minded fans in the world deserve.

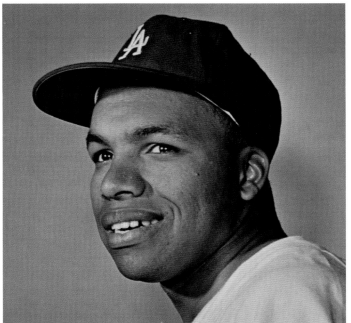

ABOVE *(Clockwise from top left)* Pitchers Don Sutton, Claude Osteen and Bill Singer (Sutton and Osteen switched gloves for photo); 1965 teammates Ron Fairly, Lou Johnson and Bob Miller; Al Ferrara greets former Dodger Maury Wills in Spring Training, 1967; Tommy Davis won consecutive NL batting titles in 1962 and 1963. **OPPOSITE** 1966 Unocal promotional 45 rpm record featuring catcher John Roseboro on the sleeve; outfielder Frank Howard.

World Series. I was fortunate enough to win the batting title, Wills was stealing all those bases and Don Drysdale won 25 games. But the end of the 1962 season still bothers me. We had a three-game lead with one week remaining and a three-game series at home with Houston and St. Louis. Houston was an expansion team in 1962; they were first called the Colt .45s before being renamed the Astros. Whatever they were called back then, I can't believe they beat us two out of three. The Cardinals came to town and beat us in three consecutive close games, and San Francisco forced a playoff. We were winning 4–2 in the ninth inning of the third and deciding playoff game, but the Giants rallied for four runs and won the game, 6–4.

We came back and won the World Series in 1963. Going back to Spring Training, we didn't dwell on blowing the pennant to the Giants. We had a businesslike attitude. You can't play good baseball if you're mad. We came back and knew what we had to do. You find out who's pitching on the other team and go over the scouting reports—things like what they like to throw you with

two strikes in the count. You do the whole cycle over again, and this time, in 1963, we were the best team.

With a pitching staff that included Drysdale, Sandy Koufax, Johnny Podres and Ron Perranoski, a team couldn't pitch any better than we did in the World Series against the New York Yankees. It was the best thing I've ever seen in my life. Because I'm from Brooklyn, all my friends from New York were happy. Koufax struck out 15 in the first game at Yankee Stadium and won, 5–2. Podres won the second game, and Drysdale won, 1–0, in the third game. Koufax finished them off in the fourth game and we won, 2–1, to win the title.

As a kid, I always loved the Dodgers and hated the Yankees. However, by the time I was old enough to be scouted as a big league prospect, most of the attention was coming from the Yankees. They really seemed to like me. In fact, I even had a locker at Yankee Stadium and could work out with the team as often as I wanted. I probably would've signed with the Yankees if I hadn't gotten a phone call from Jackie Robinson. It was

John Roseboro
TALKS
WITH
Vin Scully

Robinson who told me what the Dodger organization was like, and he made it sound like a family situation, which it was. He also told me if I had the ability to play Major League ball, the Dodgers wouldn't hesitate in giving me a chance.

Looking back, I was excited to be in my first World Series. Willie Davis was my roommate, and we were going to do our thing in the Series. You couldn't ask for anything better. The Yankees were in the World Series seven times against the Dodgers in the 1940s and 1950s but could only win one time, in 1955. This was great for me to be on a team that beat the Yankees. When the Series was finally over, I was happy and thankful, and I loved everyone. I didn't like champagne that much, but I drank plenty after our victory. Everything was perfect at that time.

It was quite a time to be a young player on a championship team and have movie stars coming to the ballpark. We all had a chance to be on television shows, and we even performed onstage in Las Vegas. Imagine having a

two-week engagement at the Sands Hotel with teammates like Davis, Drysdale, Howard, Perranoski and Moose Skowron. We were movie stars and had to join the actors' unions to perform. Even Leo Durocher, a coach at the time, was on shows like *The Munsters* and *Mister Ed*. Leo knew everyone in town, he loved people and he loved to talk. Walter Alston, the manager, was totally different. He was from a small town in Ohio and was very quiet. I understood him and liked him as well.

I left the Dodgers after the 1966 season. We had some great ballplayers in that era. Look at some of the opponents during the decade—guys like Frank Robinson, Willie Mays, Bob Gibson, Tom Seaver and Hank Aaron. There were only 12 teams in each league, so there were a lot of good minor league players who couldn't break through. I was lucky to get a chance with the Dodgers.

Tommy Davis *played with the Dodgers from 1959 to 1966 and won the National League batting title in 1962 and 1963. He set the Dodgers' single-season record for RBI (153) in 1962.*

Stadium construction revealed the main seating bowl carved into the hillside.

Dodger Stadium Construction

The groundbreaking ceremony at Chavez Ravine on September 17, 1959, finally gave Dodger President Walter O'Malley the canvas he desired to orchestrate his dream ballpark. But turning the vision into a reality proved challenging because the site featured a network of washes, gullies and gulches that were interlaced with hills and twisting roads. More than 8 million cubic yards of earth were moved to reshape the area.

Instead of building Dodger Stadium on flat ground, O'Malley and architect Emil Praeger wanted to take advantage of the landscape and decided to carve the main seating bowl from the hillside. The northern face of the rock-and-sandstone hill was cut into a rough amphitheater, and benches were cut into the sloping floor to support the stadium foundations and pedestals. To control erosion, a two-inch-thick layer of concrete was sprayed over the area. The 124-foot-high grandstand had three major cantilever tiers built on 78 precast bents. The actual construction of Dodger Stadium didn't begin until Labor Day 1960, which left only 19 months to move the remaining 5.5 million yards of dirt en route to building the stadium.

On September 3, 1959, a $646,890 contract for grading the site of Dodger Stadium was awarded by Los Angeles' Board of Public Works to Alhambra's Vinnell Constructors. The company specialized in municipal projects involving large amounts of concrete, including freeway interchanges. O'Malley surprised Vinnell executives when he asked if they could build the ballpark using Praeger's designs; O'Malley wanted the structure made of concrete instead of steel. On August 25, 1960, O'Malley signed a contract with Vinnell for the entire construction of the ballpark. Part of the deal specified that Vinnell's Jack Yount would personally supervise the building to avoid potential delays with subcontractors. It would also be the first privately financed stadium since Yankee Stadium, which was built by a brewery in 1923.

A six-acre casting yard was built by Vinnell with concrete casting beds three inches thick, 50 feet wide and between 200 and 400 feet long. Vinnell cast the 22-foot-long seat units in steel side forms and cured them with steam. All other concrete members were cast in wood forms and covered with curling compound. The casting yard was used because of the available space and because some of the members, including the 32-ton frames, were too large to truck into the site. More than 25,000 pieces were used to build the ballpark, and each piece of concrete was marked and catalogued so the erection crew could find it. Fiberglass molds were used instead of steel, and a special $150,000 one-time-use crane was assembled at the stadium to put the pieces into place.

As the stadium began to take shape, the Dodgers announced in June 1961 that it would have 52,000 seats and could be expanded in stages to boost capacity to 67,000 and eventually 80,000. O'Malley finally settled on a 56,000-seat capacity.

OPPOSITE Dick Walsh, *right*, discussed stadium construction with fellow Dodger Vice President Fresco Thompson.
ABOVE RIGHT Commemorative box distributed at the groundbreaking ceremony so fans could take home dirt as a souvenir.

GRAND OPENING
APRIL 10, 1962

46
AISLE

A
BOX

3
SEAT

FIELD BOX

PARK IN ANY ODD

NUMBERED **YELLOW** LOT

LOS ANGELES

Dodgers

VERSUS

CINCINNATI REDS

DODGER STADIUM

EST. PR. $3.27
FED. TAX .23

TOTAL $3.50

OPENING DAY
DODGER STADIUM

APRIL 10, 1962
1:00 P.M.

LOS ANGELES
Dodgers
VERSUS
CINCINNATI REDS

$3.50

EST. PR. $3.27
FED. TAX .23

ADMIT ONE

SEE OVER
FOR CONDITIONS

FIELD BOX

AISLE

LOS ANGELES
Dodgers

OUR NEW HOME AT

Dodger Stadium

IS READY

Address... 1000 ELYSIAN PARK AVENUE

LOS ANGELES 12, CALIFORNIA

TELEPHONE 225-1411

Don Drysdale

BY ANN MEYERS DRYSDALE

Southern California native Don Drysdale spent his entire Hall of Fame career (1956-1969) with the Dodgers. He appeared in five World Series and won 209 games, including 49 shutouts. In 1968, Drysdale set Major League records with six consecutive shutouts and 58⅔ scoreless innings. Drysdale returned to the Dodgers as a broadcaster in 1988 and remained a popular fixture at the ballpark until his passing at age 56 during the 1993 season.

What would I like people to remember about Don? The biggest thing is that he was a competitor. He came to play every day. As competitive as he was, off the field he could be your best friend. Don never talked about himself. He just talked about the games he played in. We are blessed that there is so much information out there about Don, because he was a public figure. I love it when people tell me, "Your husband did this . . ." and relay a story about how Don affected their lives.

Even when Don wasn't having a good day as a player, his demeanor could make others play hard. He had a great sense of humor, like in the first game of the 1965 World Series in Minnesota when Sandy Koufax sat out because of Yom Kippur. The Twins bombed Don, and when Walter Alston came to the pitcher's mound to replace him, Don said, "I'll bet you wish I was Jewish." Another time an umpire checked for Brylcreem in his hair, and Don said, "Usually I get kissed when someone does that to me."

But Don also had courage and strength and wasn't concerned with the consequences. His rule was "If you hit one of my batters, I'm going to hit two of yours." He always backed up his teammates. When opposing batters hit a home run, they didn't look at Don. They ran around the bases fast.

Today, it's hard to keep my emotions in check when I visit the stadium. When [our daughter] Drew was singing the national anthem in 2011, in my heart I was wishing Don could be there to share in the moment. I also thought, "Thank goodness she has her father's voice." She walked up the aisle after singing, and someone wearing a No. 53 Dodger jersey asked for her signature. She told me, "Mom, that's my first autograph!"

The kids are older now, and they see the pictures and hear the stories. But in a sense, they didn't know who their father was. D.J. relates the most because he's the oldest and was born on Don's birthday. It hurts to hear Darren say he didn't know his dad, and Drew was just 2½ months old when Don passed away. They would've loved to have a guy like him around and teaching them many things as a father.

Ann Meyers Drysdale *is the widow of Don Drysdale, whom she married in 1986. She has raised the couple's three children: sons D.J. and Darren and daughter Drew.*

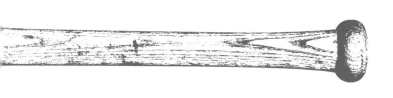

Red Patterson

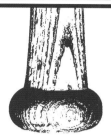

Arthur E. "Red" Patterson (1909-1992) enjoyed the best of both worlds during his 65-year association with professional baseball. After spending his first two decades chasing stories as a newspaper reporter for the New York Herald Tribune, Patterson became the standard for front office public relations excellence with the New York Yankees, the Brooklyn/Los Angeles Dodgers and the California Angels.

Patterson was covering the Yankees in 1939 when he broke the story that ailing first baseman Lou Gehrig was going to bench himself after playing in a record 2,130 consecutive games. His other big scoop occurred by accident during his daily offseason call in 1942 to Brooklyn Dodger executive Jim Mulvey. When Patterson called the ballpark, he was cut into a telephone conversation between Mulvey's wife and the telephone operator, who was also Jim Mulvey's secretary. Patterson kept his hand over the mouthpiece and soon heard that Branch Rickey was going to take over the Dodgers as team president.

After one year as the National League's public relations director, Patterson joined the Yankees in 1946 as the sport's first team publicist. Patterson introduced the concept of a yearbook for fans and a media guide for the reporters. Behind the scenes, Patterson planned publicity and marketing campaigns like a Hollywood director, arranging photo shoots and pitching stories. In 1948, he staged the first Old-Timers' Day at Yankee Stadium as a way to honor Babe Ruth. Patterson also suggested the first cap day promotion, even though Yankees General Manager George Weiss wasn't sold on the idea.

"I don't want every kid in New York wearing a Yankees cap," he said.

Patterson replied, "George, what could be better? That's the greatest ad you could have."

When the Yankees' Mickey Mantle hit a home run out of Washington's Griffith Stadium in 1953, Patterson left the ballpark and located the spot where the ball landed with a measuring tape. Patterson returned to the press box and announced the ball had traveled 565 feet, which became the first "tape measure home run."

Patterson joined the Dodgers in 1954, just in time to watch Brooklyn win its first championship the following season. During Spring Training in 1957, Patterson dealt with two sets of media—the skeptical New York scribes expecting the Dodgers to move, and the excited Los Angeles writers hoping they indeed would leave Brooklyn. Whether in Brooklyn or Los Angeles, Patterson's passion for the game made him a favorite within the industry. During his prime, he averaged 300 speeches a year to service clubs and community groups.

With the New York Yankees in 1953, publicist Red Patterson made Mickey Mantle's home run out of Washington's Griffith Stadium famous by announcing a "tape-measured" distance of 565 feet.

LOS ANGELES
Dodgers

LOS ANGELES
DODGER STADIUM

1962 OFFICIAL DO

SCOR

Sandy Koufax

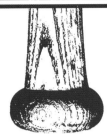

When Sandy Koufax was elected to the Baseball Hall of Fame in 1972, sportswriters asked him to look back on his career, an unusual request of someone just 36 years old. Following a 27-win season in 1966, Koufax retired because of arthritis, closing one of the most remarkable chapters in baseball history.

Koufax signed with the Brooklyn Dodgers in December 1954. Because of his bonus, a rule at the time required Koufax to stay on the Major League roster. Koufax never pitched in the minor leagues, so his on-the-job training began at age 19 with the 1955 World Championship team.

In 12 seasons, Koufax compiled a 165-87 record and a 2.76 ERA. A three-time Cy Young Award winner and National League MVP in 1963, Koufax was also the MVP of the 1963 and 1965 World Series. He led the NL in ERA in five consecutive seasons from 1962 to 1966 and in 1965 set a single-season record with 382 strikeouts. He pitched four no-hitters, including the only perfect game in Dodger history against the Chicago Cubs on September 9, 1965.

So, which game did Koufax choose as his most memorable? His first 18-strikeout game against the San Francisco Giants during the 1959 pennant race? The record-setting 15 strikeouts against the Yankees in Game 1 of the 1963 World Series at Yankee Stadium? The 2–0 shutout in the deciding Game 7 of the 1965 World Series at Minnesota's Metropolitan Stadium?

Koufax picked the final day of the 1966 regular season when the pennant race between the Dodgers, the San Francisco Giants and the Pittsburgh Pirates still was undecided. By losing the first game of a doubleheader against the Phillies, 4–3, the Dodgers went into the nightcap with a one-game lead against the Giants. San Francisco had eliminated the Pirates with a 7–3 victory in 11 innings at Forbes Field. If the Dodgers lost the second game against Philadelphia, the Giants would have trailed by one half game and flown to Cincinnati to make up a rained-out game. If the Giants won that game, they would face the Dodgers in a playoff.

Pitching on two days' rest, Koufax opposed Philadelphia right-hander Jim Bunning, in search of his 20th victory. The Dodgers jumped on Bunning for four runs in five innings, including a two-run home run by Willie Davis during a three-run third inning. Koufax scattered four hits in the first eight innings and held a 6–0 lead entering the ninth. But the Phillies didn't go quietly in the ninth. An error, two singles and a two-run double by Bill White cut the deficit to 6–3. With a runner on second and no outs, Koufax struck out Bob Uecker, retired pinch-hitter Bobby Wine on a groundout and fanned Jackie Brandt to end the game.

In the clubhouse, the champagne flowed as the Los Angeles players looked forward to a World Series against the Baltimore Orioles. The Dodgers didn't realize they were also celebrating Koufax's final victory.

OPPOSITE Sandy Koufax's fourth no-hitter, a 1–0 masterpiece against the Chicago Cubs on September 9, 1965 at Dodger Stadium, remains the only perfect game ever by a Dodger pitcher.

Chicago CUBS
s. Los Angeles DODGERS

THU.
SEP. 9 1965

8:00 P.M.

GER STADIUM   LOS ANGELES

EST. PR. $2.36
FED. TAX   .14 TOTAL $2.50

ADMIT ONE — Subject to t
set forth on th

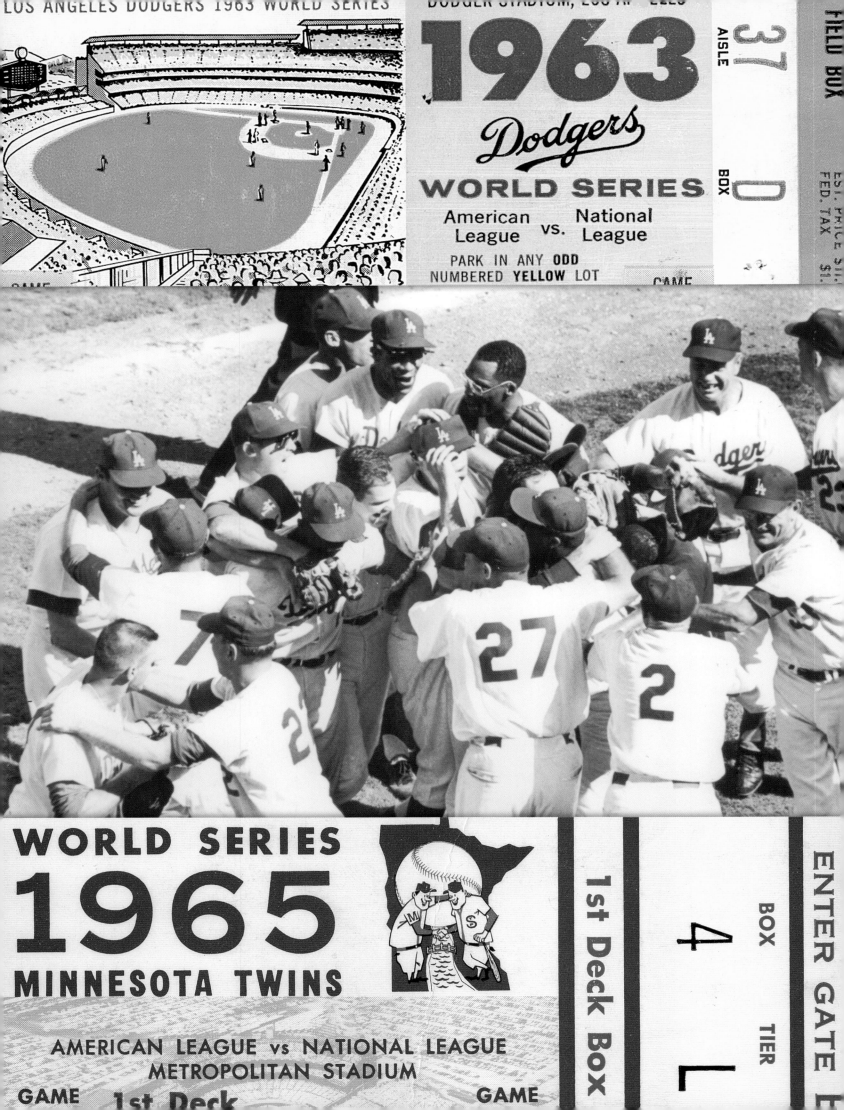

The Dynasty

When the Dodgers lost the 1962 National League playoffs against the San Francisco Giants, wasting a 4–2 lead in the ninth inning of the third and deciding game, Dodger Owner Walter O'Malley sent special handkerchiefs to season ticket customers with a stitched message: We won't blow it next year.

During the next four seasons, the Dodgers parlayed pitching, speed and defense into three World Series appearances and two championships. From 1963 to 1966, Hall of Fame pitchers Sandy Koufax and Don Drysdale combined for 170 victories, 158 complete games and 49 shutouts.

The 1963 Dodgers won 99 games during the regular season and won the pennant by six games over the St. Louis Cardinals. Tommy Davis captured his second consecutive NL batting crown with a .326 average, and Frank Howard provided the power with 28 home runs. Shortstop Maury Wills, who stole a record 104 bases in 1962, averaged 56 stolen bases from 1963 to 1966.

The Fall Classic of 1963 gave the Dodger franchise a measure of "October revenge" against the New York Yankees, a team against which the Dodgers had gone 1-6 in seven World Series between 1941 and 1956. The Dodgers swept New York in four games, the first time the Yankees had ever been whitewashed in a World Series. During a 5–2 victory in the opener at Yankee Stadium, Koufax set a single-game record with 15 strikeouts. Johnny Podres and Ron Perranoski combined on a 4–1 victory in the second game, followed by Drysdale's 1–0 victory in Game 3 at Dodger Stadium. Koufax wrapped up the title with a 2–1 victory in Game 4, the first and only time the Dodgers clinched a championship on their home field.

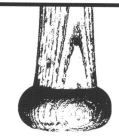

After the 1964 Dodgers finished at 80-82 and in sixth place, the 1965 team underwent changes that began with Howard being traded to the Washington Senators in a deal for pitcher Claude Osteen. Tommy Davis broke his ankle on May 1, and the Dodgers promoted outfielder Lou Johnson from Triple-A Spokane. At age 32, Johnson became an unlikely catalyst for the 1965 team, batting .259 in 131 games with 12 home runs and 58 RBI. Second baseman Jim Lefebvre won Rookie of the Year honors, batting .250 in 157 games with 12 home runs and 69 RBI. The Dodgers went 15-1 down the stretch in September to win the NL pennant by two games over San Francisco. In the World Series, the Twins beat Drysdale and Koufax in the first two games, but Osteen saved the team with a 5–0 shutout in Game 3 at Los Angeles. The Dodgers eventually won the Series in seven games.

The 1966 Dodgers entered September in third place and three games behind the Giants and the Pittsburgh Pirates. Los Angeles pitching posted a 2.03 ERA in September as the Dodgers went 20-9 for the month and won the pennant by one and a half games over the Giants. In the World Series, the Dodgers finally ran out of gas. The underdog Baltimore Orioles posted a four-game sweep by scores of 5–2, 6–0, 1–0 and 1–0 as Los Angeles was blanked over the final 33 innings.

OPPOSITE The Dodgers celebrated winning the 1963 World Series at Dodger Stadium over the New York Yankees.
ABOVE An illustartion of the championship ring, etched with the scores of the four-game sweep: 5–2, 4–1, 1–0 and 2–1.

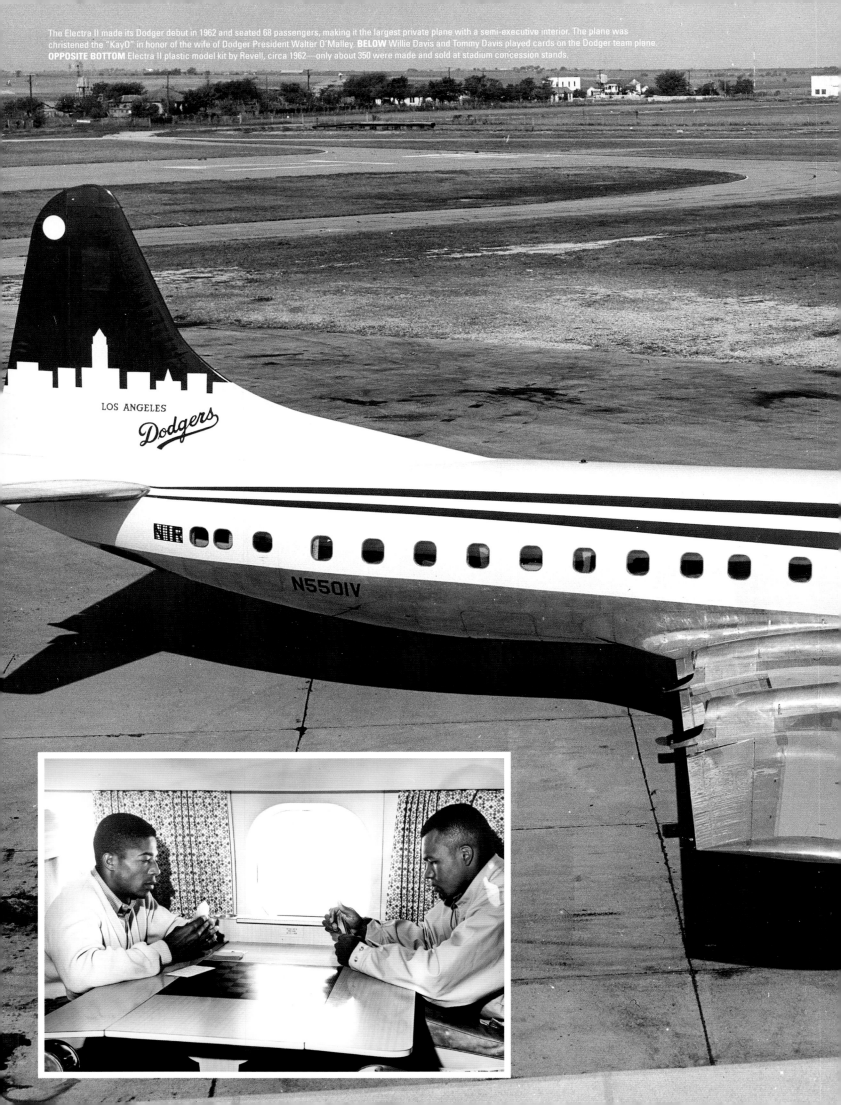

The Electra II made its Dodger debut in 1962 and seated 68 passengers, making it the largest private plane with a semi-executive interior. The plane was christened the "KayO" in honor of the wife of Dodger President Walter O'Malley. **BELOW** Willie Davis and Tommy Davis played cards on the Dodger team plane. **OPPOSITE BOTTOM** Electra II plastic model kit by Revell, circa 1962—only about 350 were made and sold at stadium concession stands.

LOS ANGELES
Dodgers

N5501V

Mexico

I n 1957, a group of youngsters from Monterrey, Mexico became the first team from outside the United States to win the Little League World Series, as Angel Macias pitched a perfect game to defeat La Mesa, California, 4-0. After their triumph in Williamsport, Pennsylvania, the Monterrey team met President Dwight David Eisenhower at the White House and then spent a day with the Brooklyn Dodgers at Ebbets Field.

More than 50 years later, in 2009, the surviving members of the Monterrey team visited the Dodgers. This time, the destination was Los Angeles' Dodger Stadium. So many things had changed since the Dodgers' first encounter with the baseball team from Mexico.

The Los Angeles Dodgers played exhibition games in Mexico during Spring Training in 1964, 1991 and 2003. The 1991 exhibition in Monterrey was the most famous, as two pitchers from Mexico—Fernando Valenzuela (Los Angeles Dodgers) and Ted Higuera (Milwaukee Brewers)—squared off for their respective Major League teams. Valenzuela was at the end of his playing career with the Dodgers, but it was an opportunity for him to pitch in his native country for the first time since 1979.

In his 10 years with the Dodgers, Valenzuela had become a national hero. His sensational 1981 rookie season, including five shutouts in his first eight starts, triggered Fernandomania throughout the United States, Mexico and Canada. Valenzuela was the box office draw Dodger President Walter O'Malley had dreamed of when the Dodgers moved to the West Coast in 1958. Valenzuela continued pitching in the Majors until 1997, and he returned to the Dodgers as a broadcaster in 2003.

During their 2009 visit to Dodger Stadium, the 1957 Monterrey Little Leaguers assembled in a large conference room and studied the personal scrapbooks of Hall of Fame catcher Roy Campanella. While 1957 had turned out to be the Dodgers' final season in Brooklyn, it was also Campanella's last appearance as a player. He was paralyzed in an automobile accident prior to the 1958 season. Campanella's scrapbooks, compiled by his mother, documented the catcher's winter ball career in Mexico: Campanella played for the Monterrey Sultanes in 1942 and 1943. Campanella's manager, Lazaro Salazar, predicted Campanella would one day play in the Majors, although the color barrier had not yet been broken. Most of the clippings were from Mexico newspapers, and the Monterrey Little Leaguers remembered meeting Campanella and asking about his days in their hometown.

In 2011, a team from Mexicali reached the international championship game of the Little League World Series at Williamsport, Pennsylvania. At Dodger Stadium, in the same conference room visited by the Monterrey Little Leaguers, a familiar figure in Dodger history sat in front of a telephone for a conference call with the latest Little League heroes. Although still modest and soft spoken, the player answered questions and gave encouraging words for their upcoming game. And although he couldn't see their faces, Valenzuela nevertheless broke into a big grin after hearing the same excited salutations: "Hola, Fernando!"

RIGHT Roy Campanella posed with a member of the Little League Baseball champions from Monterrey, Mexico during the summer of 1957 at Ebbets Field. Members of that team revisited the Dodgers at Dodger Stadium in 2009.

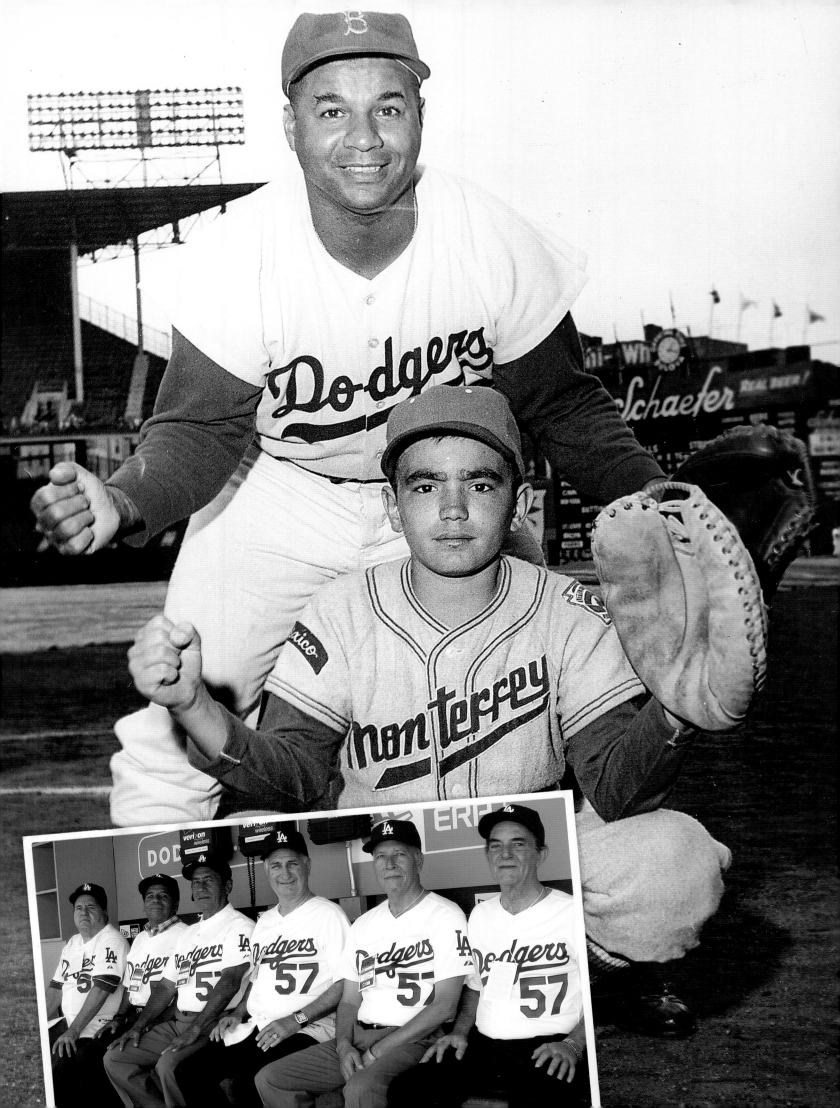

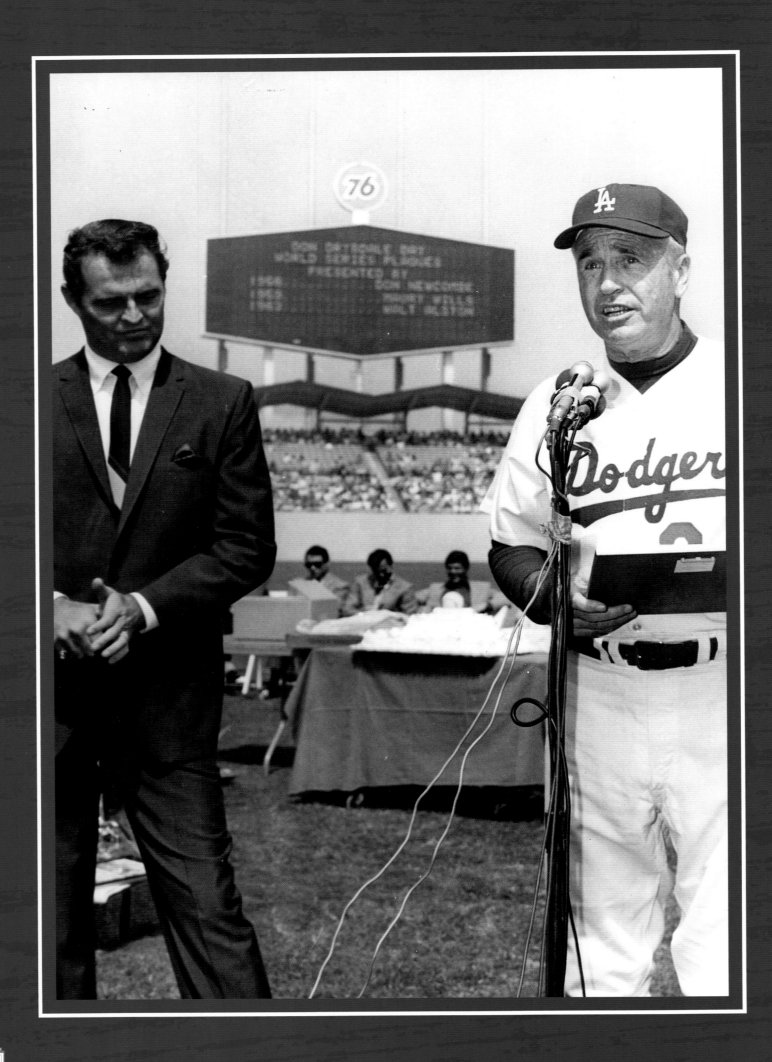

Walter Alston

BY WES PARKER

Ohio native Walter Alston piloted the Brooklyn and Los Angeles Dodgers for 23 seasons, from 1954 to 1976. Alston won four championships and seven National League pennants and was elected to the Baseball Hall of Fame in 1983.

I thought Walt was a very calm man, self-contained and sure of himself, like Teddy Roosevelt's famous saying "Speak softly and carry a big stick." Walt had to be like that if he was going to have guys like former big league managers Charlie Dressen and Leo Durocher on his coaching staff. Walt's quiet strength would come out in team meetings. People ask, "What made him so great?" One of the things was his timing. He always had his finger on the emotional pulse of the team. Walt was not a "micromanager." He was a "loose" manager, yet he had control. He'd write your name in the lineup and turn you loose. We went over the detail work in Spring Training—he organized those extremely well—so we knew what he wanted out of us. By the time the season started, there were no questions. Everything was known.

The thinking behind it was you're a man, and you're a professional, so you don't need a pep talk. You're supposed to go out and do your job. You might think that's not advantageous, but I got to the point where I became responsible for myself because of that. And I didn't look for outside help, except from within the team, among the players. I learned self-discipline from Walt, and I played up to his expectations.

Within the Dodgers, Walter Alston, Buzzie Bavasi and Walter O'Malley were like one in terms of their thinking and working together. I'm sure sometimes Walt came to the stadium and walked into Bavasi's or O'Malley's office to talk about any potential problems with the team, and they would quickly clear it up. There were some problems with a few of the players, but you always have that with guys who aren't getting a lot of playing time. They think they should be playing. Dick Stuart, a first baseman we acquired during the 1966 season, thought he should be playing instead of me during the World Series.

I've heard Casey Stengel say the secret to managing is to keep the 10 guys who hate you away from the 15 guys who don't. And there's a lot of truth to that. I think Walt did a good job of keeping the players comfortable and happy.

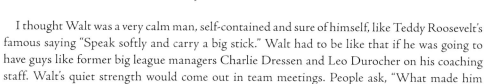

Wes Parker *is a six-time Gold Glove Award-winning first baseman who spent his entire career with the Los Angeles Dodgers, from 1964 to 1972. Walter Alston was his only Major League manager.*

THE 1960s

OPPOSITE Walter Alston gave a speech on Don Drysdale Day in 1969. **ABOVE** Alston won 2,040 regular season games during his 23 seasons as Dodger manager from 1954 to 1976.

135

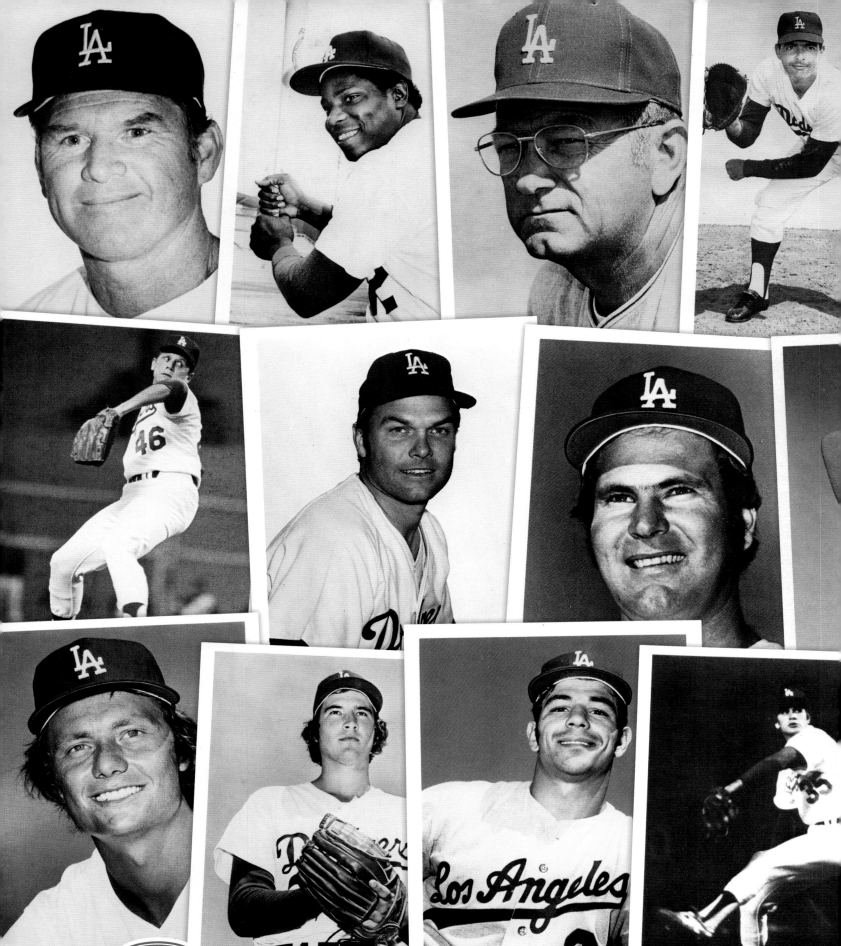

LOS ANGELES
Dodgers
PLAYER PICTURES
Autographed
20 INDIVIDUAL PICTURES

Sustained Excellence

BY RON CEY

At the start of the 1970s, the Dodgers had a nucleus of promising young players. A lot of them were from the 1968 amateur draft and were really being counted on to be part of the success the organization was hoping to have during the decade. Our Triple-A team at Albuquerque won the Pacific Coast League championship in 1972. There were more than 10 new players who came in for the next era, along with other players who arrived a little earlier, like Bill Russell, Bill Buckner and Steve Garvey.

Tommy Lasorda also joined the Dodgers as a coach in 1973. He was an important part of the young players coming in because of his relationship with us in the minor leagues, winter ball and the instructional league. He was a prime person to have in that spot, so if there were any issues or rough patches for the young Dodger players, Tommy or Monty Basgall, another coach who had been a minor league manager, could smooth things over. Tommy and Monty knew us a lot better than Walter Alston did at the time.

It was a very interesting period. There were so many players, and there was kind of a reshuffling of positions. We were converting Russell and Davey Lopes from the outfield to the infield. Lee Lacy started the 1973 season at second base, and we had acquired Ken McMullen, a veteran third baseman, in a trade with the California Angels. We were all part of the new shaping of the team.

Our biggest competition in the National League West during the 1970s was the Cincinnati Reds. It seemed whoever went to the World Series came from our division. With all due respect to the NL East, the Phillies and the Pirates in particular, the West was where it was

going on. We knew we had our work cut out for us, but it was an interesting and challenging time with respect to putting our team together.

The formation of the record-setting infield in June 1973 came through experimentation. Buckner started the season playing first base after Wes Parker retired. Von Joshua was going to play left field, and Lopes was going to play second base in front of Lacy. I was going to take over third base, and Russell was the shortstop. But then Joshua got hurt and Buckner moved to left field. Garvey came in and started playing first base. There were all kinds of combinations of things that went on. We had Joe Ferguson and Steve Yeager behind the plate. Besides Joshua, we had Tom Paciorek, another outfielder. And the next year in 1974, came Jimmy Wynn in a trade with Houston to replace Willie Davis in center field. There were a lot of things going on early that formed this club and got us into the first of four World Series.

The first year as a group, we won 95 games in 1973 and finished 3½ games behind the Reds. Cincinnati played lights-out over the final 50 games of the season. It was disappointing not being able to hold onto the lead

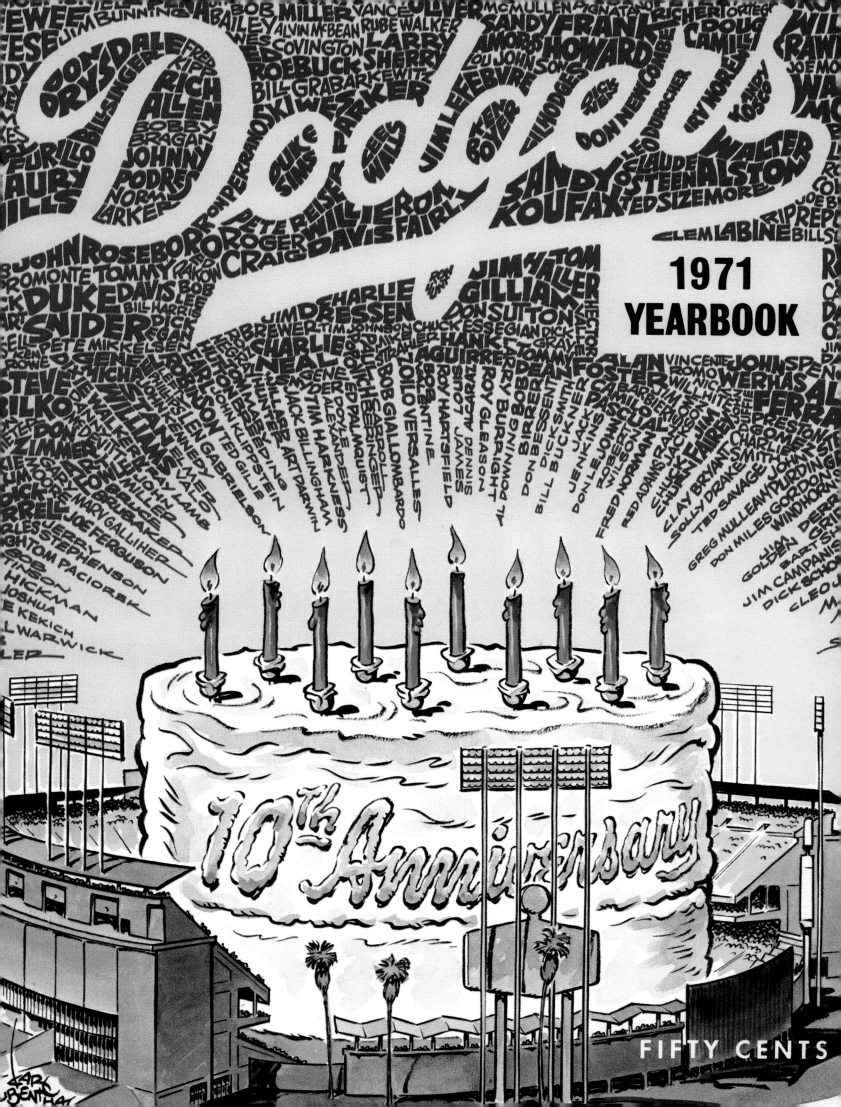

ABOVE First baseman Wes Parker won six consecutive Gold Glove Awards from 1967 to 1972, and in 2007 he was named to the all-time Rawlings Gold Glove team. **OPPOSITE TOP** During the 1972 Old-Timers' Day ceremonies in 1972, the Dodgers retired the first three uniform numbers in club history: Jackie Robinson (42), Roy Campanella (39) and Sandy Koufax (32). **OPPOSTIE BOTTOM** The early-season infield of 1972 included *(left to right)* third baseman Steve Garvey, shortstop Bill Russell, second baseman Bobby Valentine and first baseman Bill Buckner.

too good." It made it feel like we played great. Ninety-five wins is usually enough to get you into the playoffs, so it set the stage for the next year and gave us a lot of confidence.

We were able to win 102 games and the divisional title in 1974. In the NLCS, we played Pittsburgh, which had given us trouble during the regular season. We had two trips into Pittsburgh and went 0-6, which is a little strange for a team that wins 102 games. We started the playoffs on the road, and there was a little bit of talk like, "Hey, you guys haven't won here. Is that going to be a problem?" As it turned out, it wasn't. We won the first two games of the playoffs and won the series in four games.

Walt Alston was the one at the end of the 1974 World Series who said he was very proud of us. He didn't want us to feel badly about losing to Oakland, the reigning World Champions, in five games. He felt confident we'd be back in the World Series. That prophecy turned out to be correct, although it was not under his reign.

Tommy Lasorda took over from Walt at the end of the 1976 season. Tommy and Walter were really polar opposites. Walt was very quiet and shy and took care of business behind the scenes. Tommy was very open, hugging his players, with open admiration for what they were doing. They both got their jobs done very well in a different way. When it was Walt's time to be finished as the manager, Tommy was probably the best choice to take over, because he had all of us in the minor leagues.

In Tommy's first season in 1977, we got off to a 17-3 start in April and had a pretty large lead after the first 20 games. At the end of May, it ballooned up to more than 10 games. The rest of the season was pretty much in the bag, and people knew it was over. As much as we had to finish the season, there wasn't much of a difference in what we had built up the first months of the season. I don't know if that was a good thing or a bad thing. I personally didn't feel like I was going into the postseason on a high note, even though statistically I had some of my better numbers. We lost to the Yankees in six games in the World Series.

The 1978 season was different because we really needed to push it down the stretch. There was a time in

we had during the summer. But it wasn't so much that we lost the division; rather, the Reds won it. There's a different way to approach things sometimes, when you analyze things. I think I would've felt worse if we had crumbled and played 10 games under .500 during the final month. My recollection is that we played pretty well, but Cincinnati was just too much to handle.

Looking at it with that perspective gave us a better feeling: "Hey, we had a great season. Cincinnati was just

early August we were maybe five games back. From that point on, we played great baseball for the last month and a half. We went into the playoffs on a high note. Once again, we took care of the Phillies in the NLCS in four games. We ended up clinching the pennant at Dodger Stadium, and I had scored the winning run on Bill Russell's base hit to center field. It propelled us into the 1978 World Series, which turned into a disappointing and heartbreaking loss to the Yankees. I felt the Series got away from us because of an umpire's call on an interference play in New York.

At this point, we've been in three World Series and I'm thinking, "We've got to finish this off." We were too good a team not to win a championship. We were playing great baseball and were one of the elite teams in the Majors. We still had a lot left.

Ron Cey played for the Dodgers from 1971 to 1982 and was a six-time All-Star. Cey not only won his elusive World Series in 1981 but was also named World Series tri-MVP.

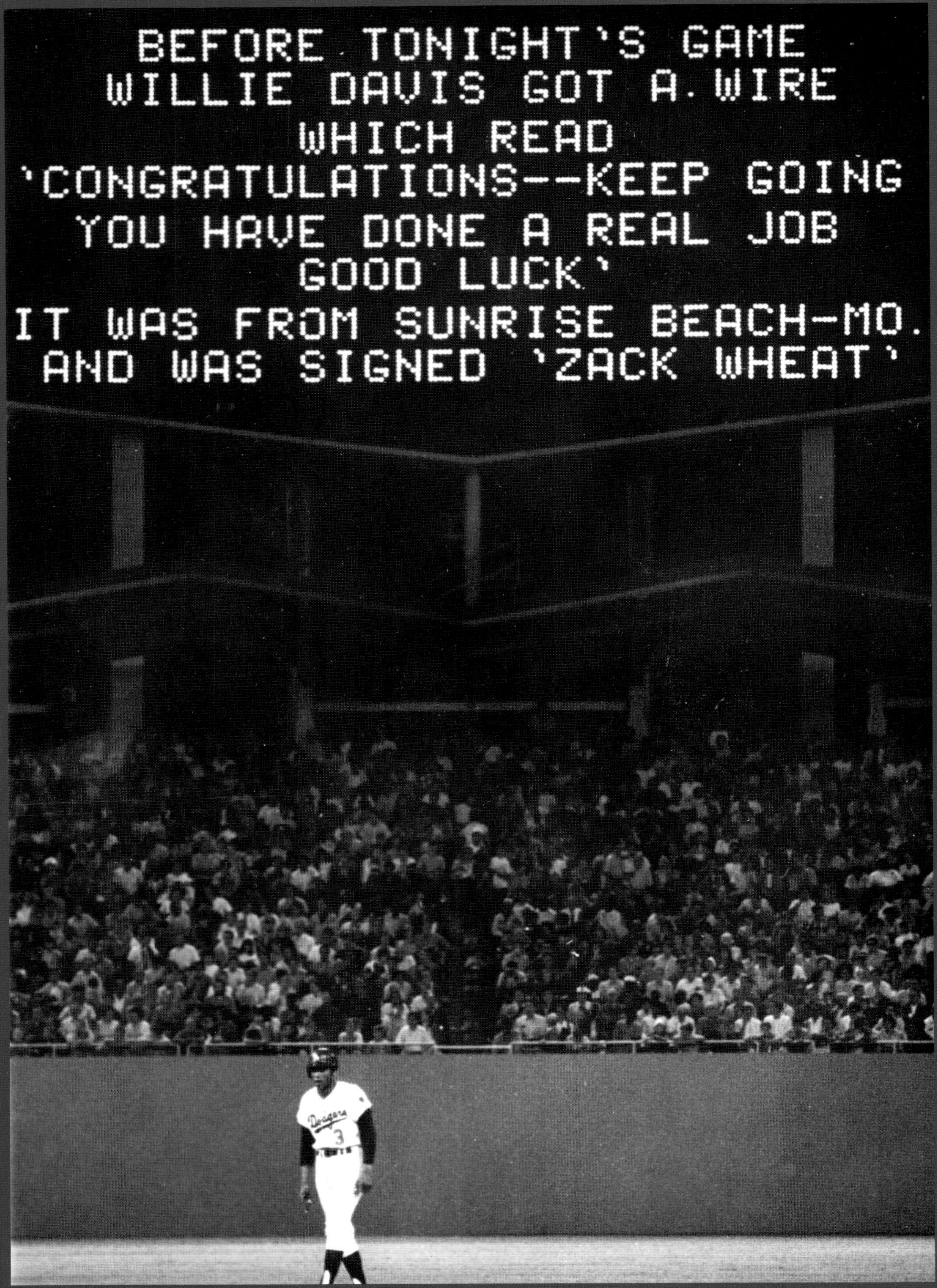
BEFORE TONIGHT'S GAME
WILLIE DAVIS GOT A WIRE
WHICH READ
'CONGRATULATIONS--KEEP GOING
YOU HAVE DONE A REAL JOB
GOOD LUCK'
IT WAS FROM SUNRISE BEACH-MO.
AND WAS SIGNED 'ZACK WHEAT'
Dodgers
3

Willie Davis

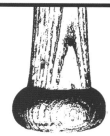

Center fielder Willie Davis became the all-time Los Angeles franchise leader in several categories with the Dodgers from 1960 to 1973, including most hits (2,091), extra-base hits (585), at-bats (7,495), runs (1,004), triples (110) and total bases (3,094). Originally a track star at Roosevelt High in Los Angeles, Davis caught the attention of Dodger scout Kenny Myers, who signed Davis to a $13,000 bonus contract in 1958. After polishing his baseball skills, Davis became a fixture with Los Angeles and appeared in three World Series. Davis, who passed away at age 69 in 2010, discussed his Dodger days during this 2007 team interview:

Putting on a Major League uniform for the first time was a unique experience, because I never imagined as a kid that I would be playing pro baseball. I was an athlete and a sprinter. I ran track in high school, but I was good in all sports. I'm pretty sure I could've been a pro in any sport I chose, whether baseball or basketball. I knew right off the bat I wasn't going to mess around with football because I had a little paper route. I was making money, $5 or $6 a day, and I wasn't going to give that up to practice football.

I didn't watch much baseball on television as a kid and I didn't really have any role models. I did my own thing. I figured if you learned and practiced the fundamentals in anything, and they are the correct fundamentals, you can't miss. You're going to be successful.

When I first attended a Dodger training camp, the young players were fundamentally sound. The Dodgers not only stressed the fundamentals, they had the guys to teach you correctly. And you loved it because it was a family atmosphere . . . Maury Wills, Wally Moon, Frank Howard, Tommy Davis, Joe Pignatano, Jim Gilliam and John Roseboro. Many people might not know them for their careers, but man, those guys were fantastic off the field.

I had so many great moments it's hard to separate them. But just being a part of the Dodger organization and learning the fundamentals—that was so much fun, too. You sensed that if you got these things done, you were going to be around. I always had that feeling from the beginning. Buzzie Bavasi, the Dodger general manager, was kind of like my father, adopting me because I was from the Los Angeles area. He knew how fast I was, but I don't think he knew how good of a hitter or a player I would be until he saw me at Spring Training. Right from the get-go, I was one of the favorites there. I was a California boy and you know I was groovin' and feeling so good about the situation. Walter Alston was giving me encouragement all the time and I always appreciated that.

PREVIOUS *(Left to right)* Pitching coach Red Adams, Burt Hooton, Don Sutton, Al Downing, manager Walter Alston, Tommy John and Doug Rau. **OPPOSITE** Willie Davis set a club record with a 31-game hitting streak in 1969, breaking Zack Wheat's record of 29 set in 1916. **ABOVE** Davis batted safely in 25 consecutive games in 1971.

Summer of 1974

The opening of Dodger Stadium in 1962 brought fans an instant, albeit heartbreaking, pennant race with the San Francisco Giants, followed by three World Series appearances over the next four seasons. Major League Baseball expanded its playoff pool from two teams to four in 1969 by dividing each league into two divisions. But after a seven-year absence from the postseason, the 1974 Dodgers captured their first NL West crown thanks to a core of young players and two veterans from other organizations.

Outfielder Jimmy Wynn, acquired from the Houston Astros in exchange for pitcher Claude Osteen, earned NL Comeback Player of the Year honors after batting .271 in 150 games with 32 home runs and 108 RBI. Right-hander Mike Marshall became the first relief pitcher in history to win the Cy Young Award. Marshall, acquired from the Montreal Expos in exchange for outfielder Willie Davis, went 15-12 with a 2.42 ERA and 21 saves. He set MLB single-season records for most appearances (106) and most innings (208.1) by a reliever.

The 1974 season also saw dominant performances by young players becoming established stars. In his first full season as the team's first baseman, Steve Garvey won NL Most Valuable

Player honors, batting .312 in 156 games, with 21 home runs and 111 RBI. Garvey also won MVP honors at the All-Star Game after being named to the starting lineup as a write-in candidate. Third baseman Ron Cey provided added power with 18 home runs and 97 RBI.

Starting pitchers Andy Messersmith (20-6) and Don Sutton (19-9) anchored a staff that led the Majors with a 2.97 ERA, despite missing Tommy John (13-3) after a season-ending elbow injury on July 17.

The Dodgers (102-60) edged the Reds (98-64) by four games to win the division after leading by as many as 10½ games on July 10. Cincinnati's last chance occurred during a weekend series in mid-September in Los Angeles. The Reds won the first two games to cut the deficit to 1½ games, but Wynn blasted a grand slam the following afternoon to spark a 7–1 victory, and Cincinnati never got closer.

In the NL Championship Series, Sutton shut down the Pittsburgh Pirates in his two starts, allowing the Dodgers to win the best-of-five series, 3-1. In 17 innings, Sutton scattered one run on seven hits.

Although the Dodgers would lose the World Series in five games against the Oakland Athletics, the nucleus was in place for more pennant races in the 1970s when either the Reds or the Dodgers won the NL West in nine of 10 seasons. Wynn and Marshall never again appeared in a World Series, and both were gone by the time Tommy Lasorda took over from longtime manager Walter Alston at the end of the 1976 season.

ABOVE Joe Ferguson and Steve Garvey celebrated the NL pennant with broadcaster Jerry Doggett. **OPPOSITE** 1974 giveaway poster.

Dodgers '74

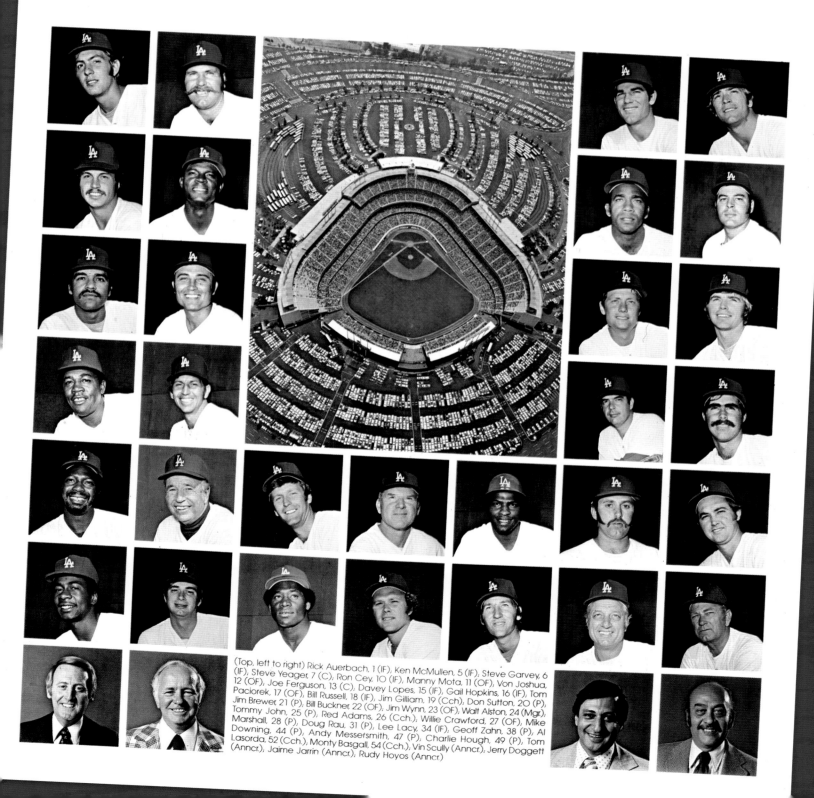

(Top, left to right) Rick Auerbach, 1 (IF), Ken McMullen, 5 (IF), Steve Garvey, 6 (IF), Steve Yeager, 7 (C), Ron Cey, 10 (IF), Manny Mota, 11 (OF), Von Joshua, 12 (OF), Joe Ferguson, 13 (C), Davey Lopes, 15 (IF), Gail Hopkins, 16 (IF), Tom Paciorek, 17 (OF), Bill Russell, 18 (IF), Jim Gilliam, 19 (Cch), Don Sutton, 20 (P), Jim Brewer, 21 (P), Bill Buckner, 22 (OF), Jim Wynn, 23 (OF), Walt Alston, 24 (Mgr), Tommy John, 25 (P), Red Adams, 26 (Cch), Willie Crawford, 27 (OF), Mike Marshall, 28 (P), Doug Rau, 31 (P), Lee Lacy, 34 (IF), Geoff Zahn, 38 (P), Al Downing, 44 (P), Andy Messersmith, 47 (P), Charlie Hough, 49 (P), Tom Lasorda, 52 (Cch), Monty Basgall, 54 (Cch), Vin Scully (Anncr), Jerry Doggett (Anncr), Jaime Jarrin (Anncr), Rudy Hoyos (Anncr).

Thanks For Shari
Major League R

The Dodgers distributed a promotional "thank you" team photo when they became the first MLB team to surpass the 3-million mark in home attendance for a season in 1978.

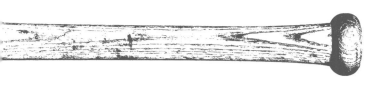

The Dodger Dog

P eanuts and Cracker Jack may be on the menu in the famous baseball song "Take Me Out to the Ball Game," but that might have changed had songwriter Jack Norworth collaborated with Thomas Arthur.

As concessions manager at Dodger Stadium in the early 1960s, Arthur wanted to borrow the concept of the foot-long hot dog from New York's Coney Island. The hot dog at Dodger games was only 10 inches, so after hearing a few fans challenge the validity of the foot-long claim, Arthur decided on the name Dodger Dog. It would become the food product most associated with a Major League team and rank alongside Vin Scully in the category of Dodger Stadium staples.

Farmer John, one of the team's main sponsors, produces the Dodger Dog, and the product is available in Southern California supermarkets. An estimated 2 million Dodger Dogs were sold at Dodger Stadium in 2011, making it the best-selling hot dog in the Majors. There also is a Dodger Dog restaurant at the Universal City Walk, adjacent to Universal Studios. And in the team's gift store, related merchandise over the years has included everything from a plastic Dodger Dog bobblehead to a stuffed fabric figurine.

Arthur's contribution to baseball history occurred after he changed career plans. He served in the U.S. Army Air Forces during World War II and wanted to become a cartoonist or illustrator when he returned home. Moonlighting while he was a student, Arthur began supplying vending machines to theaters and aircraft plants in Southern California. Eventually he won contracts to manage the concessions at the Los Angeles Memorial Coliseum, the Los Angeles Sports Arena and Chicago's Wrigley Field. Some of Arthur's drawings and other sketches were used on the early Stadium Club menus at Dodger Stadium.

The Dodgers became tenants at the Coliseum in 1958, and one of Arthur's customers might have been Norworth, a Laguna Beach resident who started that city's Little League program. The Dodgers staged a Jack Norworth Day that season, and Norworth, at age 79, sang his famous song with Scully on the pregame radio show and was honored on the field in ceremonies and presented with a trophy from the makers of Cracker Jack. Unfortunately, there is no historical reference to determine whether Norworth stayed for lunch.

OPPOSITE Dodger Stadium food concessions manager Thomas Arthur first coined the term "Dodger Dog." **RIGHT** 2002 Dodger Dog statue.

The Infield

BY TOM HOFFARTH

J une 13, 1973. Fourth inning. All four one, and one four all. Some Dodger history books note that it actually happened 10 days later, when manager Walter Alston officially wrote their names on the starting lineup card for the first time.

But after a 16–3 loss at Philadelphia, Alston had to shuffle things around, and all the pegs went in the right holes for the very first time as a unit.

Steve Garvey replaced Willie Davis in the lineup, taking over at first, which sent Tom Paciorek to center field. Rookie Davey Lopes was at second, later to replace Paciorek in the outfield. Bill Russell manned shortstop. And another rookie, Roy Cey, replacing the injured Ken McMullen, was at third.

The power of four.

Individually, they couldn't have been much more diverse: Garv, the football player from Michigan State, who embraced the spotlight like a politician with oversize forearms. Lopes, who made a living of stealing, may still be the most famous Major League Baseball player ever to come out of Providence, Rhode Island. Russell, a.k.a. "Ropes," the basketball star from Pittsburg, Kansas, who'd be the choice to someday manage the team. Cey, from Tacoma, Washington, who ran like a penguin with a white and blue tuxedo.

"But they had a common bond: they were flat-out competitors who wanted to beat your butt," said Fred Claire, the former Dodger general manager who began in the team's public relations department when the quartet was formed. "You couldn't get them out of the lineup."

Each of their careers would span more than 16 years, and their stats would more than hold their value on the backs of their baseball cards. Together, they served a greater purpose.

While much of the starting outfield and pitching staff members arrived via trades, this homegrown mesh of strength, speed and smarts showed L.A. how to achieve a common goal, year after year.

They still hold claim to maintaining the longest intact infield in Major League history— 8½ years. Tommy Lasorda's after-dinner speeches don't even last that long. And it remains a testament to their importance as the cornerstone of the Dodger teams during the 1970s and 1980s that went to four World Series in an eight-year span.

"I don't even look up their individual records when I think about them," said Claire. "They had a connection on so many fronts—first of which, was they were all great competitors who came out of the Dodgers' farm system."

Steve Garvey was an infielder without a spot to claim his own, having problems hitting the cutoff man from third base to first and committing a league-high 26 errors in 1972. But when Garvey began to settle into his role as a first baseman in 1973, everything fell into place. By 1974, he was a write-in starter for the All-Star Game, earning the MVP of not only that exhibition but also of the regular season. By the time he left the Dodgers in 1983, he had racked up eight All-Star selections and four Gold Gloves to go along with his 1974 MVP.

Davey Lopes, a 28-year-old rookie when he was called up to the Majors, also started as a center fielder before being converted to a shortstop. One of the greatest threats on the bases, he accumulated 557 career stolen bases with an astonishing 83-percent success rate, ranking third on the all-time list. In 1975, Lopes stole 38 consecutive bases without being caught and led the National League in total steals in 1975 (77) and 1976 (63).

OPPOSITE Infielders Ron Cey, Bill Russell, Davey Lopes and Steve Garvey spent 8½ seasons together from June 1973 through the 1981 World Series. **ABOVE** The foursome reunited during a preseason luncheon honoring the team's upcoming 100th anniversary.

Bill Russell was a 1966 draft pick who started as a center fielder before being converted to a shortstop by coach Monty Basgall in 1972. Russell would go on to earn three All-Star selections and man the position for the next 12 seasons, where he became the all-time leader in Dodger games played (2,181) since the team moved to the West Coast.

Ron Cey rounded out the quartet at third base, often batting cleanup while bashing 316 home runs and 1,139 RBI in his career. Known more for those home runs and RBI, he also tied a league record in 1979 with only nine errors at third. Cey was also a World Series tri-MVP (along with outfielder Pedro Guerrero and catcher Steve Yeager) in 1981, when he also won the Babe Ruth Award for postseason excellence.

Season after season, while others would start bringing in quick-fix free agents to appease impatient fans and owners, the O'Malley and Campanis brain trust allowed this group to stick it out and fulfill its baseball destiny.

But as this Dodger infield was about to clinch its first and only World Series title together, Lasorda provided the poetic ending. His lineup for what was to be the decisive Game 6 of the World Series on October 28, 1981, against the New York Yankees had Lopes, Russell, Garvey and Cey batting first through fourth. They'd finally reached the top together.

"It was kind of a storybook year," Russell was to say. "We finally won the World Series, and we beat the Yankees. We knew it might be our last hurrah together."

"It's so unique," Garvey would add. "It's a record that can't be broken, because the business has changed. You can't keep one guy for eight years, much less four."

A combined 21 All-Star Game appearances while together, five Gold Gloves, a couple of stolen-base titles, a league MVP trophy, consecutive game streaks, clutch playoff performances and even one-third of a World Series MVP trophy is what is held as a group victory.

"Tremendous pride and ability, and a bond that will always be there," said Claire. "They can't ever be separated."

Not after you'd witnessed this cherished power of four.

That's four, as in forever.

Tom Hoffarth *covers sports media for the* Los Angeles Daily News, *where he has worked since 1992.*

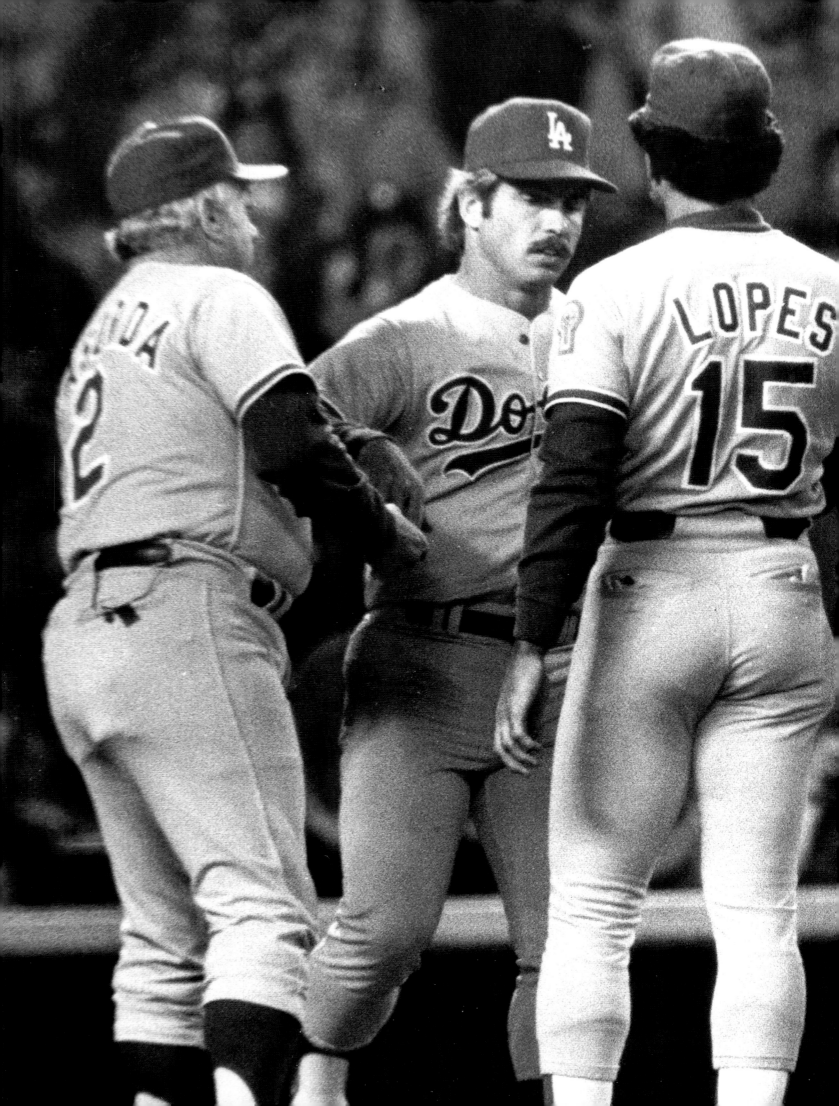

1977 and 1978 Pennants

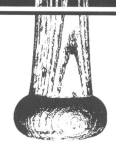

Gabby Street wouldn't register in the minds of most Dodger fans in the late 1970s, but the former St. Louis Cardinal manager put Tommy Lasorda's first two seasons in the Los Angeles dugout in historical perspective. When Lasorda's teams reached the World Series in 1977 and 1978, he and Street were the only managers in the 20th century to win National League pennants in their first two seasons, a feat Street achieved with the Cardinals in 1930 and 1931.

Lasorda technically took over for Walter Alston on September 29, 1976, and went 2-2, although those games were credited to Alston's ledger. The 1976 Dodgers (92-70) finished 10 games behind the Cincinnati Reds in the NL West. Although the Reds would win their second consecutive World Series that fall, Lasorda boldly predicted that the Big Red Machine would not beat the Dodgers again in 1977. With the exception of veterans Dusty Baker and Rick Monday, the majority of the roster had played for Lasorda at some point in the minor leagues.

When Lasorda was a coach for Alston from 1973 to 1976, Frank Sinatra promised he'd sing the national anthem for Lasorda's first game if he ever became manager. Sinatra kept his promise on Opening Day 1977, and the Lasorda era began with a 5–1 victory over the San Francisco Giants. The Dodgers roared to a 17-3 record after 20 games and never looked back. With the division race in control in late September, Lasorda even let comedian Don Rickles sit in the dugout and visit the pitcher's mound to replace reliever Elias Sosa.

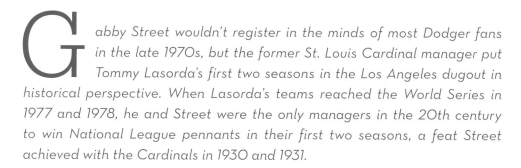

The 1977 Dodgers finished with a 98-64 record, 10 games ahead of the Reds. Steve Garvey, Reggie Smith, Ron Cey and Dusty Baker became the first quartet from the same team to each hit at least 30 home runs in one season, with respective totals of 33, 32, 30 and 30 homers. In the 1977 NL Championship Series, the Dodgers lost the first game at home, 7–5, despite Ron Cey's grand slam off Steve Carlton in the seventh inning. But Baker hit a grand slam in a 7–1 victory in Game 2. Back in Philadelphia, the Dodgers stole Game 3 with a 5–4 win, thanks to a three-run ninth inning started with a two-out bunt single by Vic Davalillo and a Manny Mota double off the glove of left fielder Greg Luzinski. In the World Series, Lasorda's dreams of a title were dashed in six games by the New York Yankees, as Reggie Jackson hit three home runs on consecutive pitches in the finale at Yankee Stadium.

The 1978 NL West race was tougher, as San Francisco joined the Reds as contenders, but the Dodgers pulled away from Cincinnati in late September to win the division by 2½ games with a 95-67 record. But the postseason produced the same results. Los Angeles defeated the Phillies, 3-1, in the NLCS and lost to the Yankees, 4-2, in the World Series.

PREVIOUS *(Left to right)* Manager Tommy Lasorda, Ron Cey, Davey Lopes, Bill Russell and Steve Garvey during the 1981 World Series Game 6 introductions—their final game together. **OPPOSITE** A 1978 NLCS program cover celebrated the team's L.A.-era pennants. **ABOVE** Catcher Steve Yeager congratulated Bob Welch after the rookie pitcher saved Game 2 of the 1978 World Series.

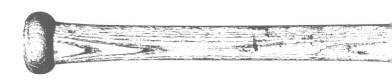

Don Sutton

BY STEVE YEAGER

R ight-hander Don Sutton spent the first 15 seasons of his 23-year career with the Dodgers from 1966 to 1980 and holds nearly every Dodger career record for Dodger pitchers, including wins (233), strikeouts (2,696), games (550), shutouts (52) and innings (3,814). Sutton returned to Los Angeles for his final season in 1988 and retired with a career mark of 324-256 and a 3.26 ERA in 774 games.

I was just a kid in 1972 when I started to catch Don Sutton, who already was an established starting pitcher with the Dodgers. He took care of me as a young player, the sign of a professional. He took time to teach me along the way, which says a lot about his character. The patience he showed with me stayed with me my whole career and helped me understand the art of calling a game.

Don was a quiet man who went about his business and always had a plan. When he pitched, you always knew your team had a chance to win. He was going to give our offense a chance to score a couple of runs and win the game. I don't ever remember him getting blown out early in a game.

Don was a guy who could do a lot of things with the baseball. He could run it in on right-handed batters and could move the ball around the plate. He had a great curve and command of all his pitches. He didn't have to rely on one "out" pitch. He had three or four pitches he could throw over the plate when he wanted to. And he could change speeds on his own. He never really let the hitter set in the batter's box and get comfortable.

The Dodgers won three pennants during the 1970s, and Don was the only starting pitcher on all three staffs. He was lights-out in the 1974 League Championship Series against the Pittsburgh Pirates. Don was always in control of his emotions. Every time I'd come to the pitcher's mound, we'd talk about how he wanted to pitch to a certain batter in a certain situation. But rarely would I talk to him about his mechanics. He knew what he wanted and was always in control.

Steve Yeager was drafted by the Dodgers in 1967 and spent 14 seasons with the team, including 1981 when he was named World Series tri-MVP. He caught Don Sutton in nine postseason games between 1974 and 1978.

CHAPTER

6

The 1980s

Miraculous Performances

BY STEVE SAX

When the Dodgers promoted me to the Majors during the 1981 season, people said I was the person who was going to break up the famous infield that had been together for so long—first baseman Steve Garvey, second baseman Davey Lopes, shortstop Bill Russell and third baseman Ron Cey. In retrospect, that time brings back good memories, because if there was any angst from that group about a new person, they never made me feel that way. Even Lopes, despite the fact we played the same position, was a class individual. He knew the writing was on the wall. But even with everything going on, he taught me a lot about stealing bases and always wanted to lend a hand. He knew I was going to be the next person to take his position, but he never let it get in the way of being a professional.

The 1981 season was a great way to start a career— getting a taste of success and playing in the postseason. I was mentored by a great bunch of people who were an example of how to win a World Series. In 1982, we were right there in the hunt for the playoffs until Joe Morgan hit the home run on the final day of the season at San Francisco. There were a lot of emotions during those first few seasons, both good memories and bad. There were a lot of fundamental things to learn, and I'm lucky I was on a great team that had a lot of veterans who could show the way and play ball the right way.

We won the division in 1983, but it was also a time of transition. Pedro Guerrero was playing third base,

and he was making errors everywhere. I was at second base and making errors everywhere. I think Pedro and I injured a lot of people by throwing the ball into the stands that season. But in the midst of all that, we still won the division and went to the playoffs. Those were the years when we could always get better. We'd get to a peak and then get knocked down. We'd hit another peak and get knocked down again. This all culminated in something that was fantastic in 1988. We still had the core of players like Mike Scioscia and Mike Marshall, who were there in the formative years and were still there by 1988.

After the 1987 season, the Dodgers signed Kirk Gibson as a free agent from the Detroit Tigers. We knew Kirk

PREVIOUS Kirk Gibson raised his arm after his pinch-hit home run gave the Dodgers a 5–4 victory in Game 1 of the 1988 World Series against the Oakland Athletics. **OPPOSITE** Rick Monday's solo home run in the top of the ninth inning at Montreal gave the Dodgers a 2–1 victory over the Expos in the decisive Game 5 of the 1981 NL Championship Series.

ABOVE General Manager Al Campanis, Los Angeles Mayor Tom Bradley and manager Tommy Lasorda rode in the 1981 World Series parade. **OPPOSITE** *(Clockwise from top left)* Baseball Commissioner Bowie Kuhn presented the 1981 World Series trophy to Campanis, Lasorda and Team President Peter O'Malley in the visitors' clubhouse at Yankee Stadium; Pedro Guerrero; Steve Sax leapt over his brother, Dave, in Spring Training; Ron Cey and Don Sutton celebrated the Dodgers' 1980 season-ending sweep of Houston to force a one-game NL West playoff; NBC broadcaster Bob Costas interviewed Kirk Gibson; Dusty Baker.

was a great competitor just by watching the clips of him playing in the 1984 playoffs and the World Series. Coming out of high school, he was one of the fastest guys in the nation. (He was drafted by the NFL coming out of Michigan State.)

There were so many special things to remember about our championship in 1988. During Orel Hershiser's streak of 59 scoreless innings, it's amazing how well everyone played on defense. When you have a pitcher who gets the ball and throws it and doesn't stand around a lot, the defense is always ready. There's a great thing about momentum—it really does rub off. When Orel was winning those games, a lot of it was because of our defense. As bad as our defense was in 1983, it had improved in 1988 to the point that our pitching and

defense really keyed our success, because we won a lot of games by scores of 2–1 and 3–2. Those are games won by defense and pitching, the cornerstones to the team.

Hershiser won the Cy Young Award, and Kirk was the MVP of the league. Who can ever forget his home run in the World Series at Dodger Stadium? I was standing in the on-deck circle when he was batting against Oakland's Dennis Eckersley. In those situations, I wasn't thinking of whether Kirk could hit a home run. I had to have the mind-set that I have to prepare to come to bat and win the game. So I'm thinking of what I can do to win the game. I thought that if he could just get on base, it would be a bonus. But then he hit the ball into the pavilion and I thought, "Something magical is happening."

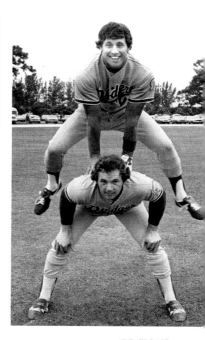

Looking back, I think beating the New York Mets in the 1988 NL Championship Series was a bigger deal than beating the Oakland Athletics in the World Series. The Mets beat us 10 out of 11 games during the regular season. (One game was washed out because of rain.) So when we beat the Mets in the seventh and deciding game at Dodger Stadium, that's when the magic started. The momentum continued into the Gibson game, and we beat the Athletics in five games.

There's one thing that I remember about winning the World Series that was pretty amazing: We ran into the clubhouse after the final game, and I went into a little side room to put my uniform in a plastic bag so it would be protected for posterity. I was sitting there by myself, and about 10 feet away, I could hear the jubilation and the yelling. Under the door, you could see the bright lights because of the television cameras. At that point, I was so mentally and physically exhausted. I could have laid down and gone to sleep, even with everything going on in the background. I would've slept for a long time, that's how exhausted I was. Being that tired and knowing we were the champions of the world, there is no better feeling. If you're a boxer or a tennis player and win a championship, you celebrate by yourself. But there is no better feeling than winning something of that magnitude as a team and being able to celebrate as a group.

Steve Sax *played for the Dodgers from 1981 to 1988, earning the NL Rookie of the Year Award in 1982. He won two World Series Championships in 1981 and 1988, and a Silver Slugger Award in 1986.*

Dodger Stadium, Game 1, 1983 NL Championship Series

1- Success Comes in Cans and not in Cants

The difference between the possible and the impossible lies in a person's determination.

The Westin Peachtree Plaza
ATLANTA
210 Peachtree Street • Atlanta, Georgia 30303 • (404) 659-1400
A Member Of The Host Hotel Network For The Atlanta Committee For The Olympic Games

I tell my players believe that you are the best; just don't tell anyone about it.

Champions are made not born.

The Westin Peachtree Plaza
ATLANTA
210 Peachtree Street • Atlanta, Georgia 30303 • (404) 659-1400
A Member Of The Host Hotel Network For The Atlanta Committee For The Olympic Games

Self Confidence is the first step to success
You will get out of life, exactly what you put into it.

There is only one route to success and that is through the one of hard work.

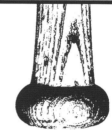

Tommy Lasorda

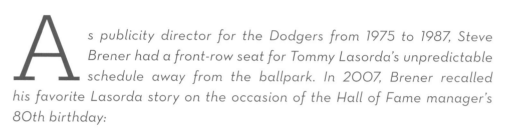

As publicity director for the Dodgers from 1975 to 1987, Steve Brener had a front-row seat for Tommy Lasorda's unpredictable schedule away from the ballpark. In 2007, Brener recalled his favorite Lasorda story on the occasion of the Hall of Fame manager's 80th birthday:

Tommy has been known to walk the streets of many National League cities after tough losses. One year, we had arrived at the Grand Hyatt Hotel in New York. The bus pulled up at about 2:30 a.m. after concluding a tough three-game series in Philadelphia. Tommy didn't want to go to bed, so he asked me to walk the streets of Manhattan with him to find a copy of the *New York Times*.

So we were walking the streets of Manhattan, heading toward the *New York Times* building to get the first morning paper. A police car pulled up and recognized Tommy and asked what we were doing. So they had us hop in, and they took us to the *Times* loading dock to get a paper and gave us a little tour of Manhattan that eventually led us to a police station located in the subway. The officers asked Tommy if he would speak to the next shift of officers coming to work that morning, and sure enough, there he was motivating the NYPD at 3 a.m.

We were about to leave a half hour later when Tommy asked the police to open up a cell where several inmates were handcuffed to the wall. Before my very eyes, Tommy went into the cell and was motivating these inmates to change their lives and do what is right for themselves, their family, their city and, most importantly, their country. The inmates were stunned that here was the Dodgers' manager, Tommy Lasorda, speaking to them in a jail cell.

Tommy signed autographs for everyone, even the inmates. We got our ride back to the Grand Hyatt Hotel, and it was probably 5 a.m. before our heads hit the pillow. And we were just going for a short walk to get a copy of the *New York Times*.

OPPOSITE Tommy Lasorda's notes for a speech in Atlanta. **ABOVE** Lasorda with his Hall of Fame plaque at Cooperstown in 1997.

Fernando Valenzuela

There will always be curiosity about the hypothetical scenario of 19-year-old rookie pitcher Fernando Valenzuela starting the one-game National League tiebreaker against the Houston Astros at the end of the 1980 season. In 10 relief appearances after his September promotion from Double-A San Antonio, Valenzuela had pitched 17⅔ scoreless innings. He had started 25 games at San Antonio but none with the Dodgers to that point. Los Angeles instead chose veteran Dave Goltz, who entered the game with a 7-10 record and a 4.28 ERA. The Astros were ahead 4-0 by the third inning and won the game, 7-1.

But if Valenzuela had started the game, chances are that the elements of Fernandomania would not have been in place in 1981 when Valenzuela came out of nowhere to become the first player in history to win both the Rookie of the Year and Cy Young awards in the same season. During Spring Training, Valenzuela was expected to be one of the candidates to join the starting rotation after the departure of longtime Dodger Don Sutton via free agency. In six exhibition games, Valenzuela went 2-1 with a 3.33 ERA. Valenzuela made the Dodger ballclub and lived with the family of scout Mike Brito, who discovered the pitcher during a 1979 Mexican League game he had attended to watch the other team's shortstop.

The Valenzuela legend began by accident in 1981. Actually, it was injuries to starting pitchers Jerry Reuss (pulled calf) and Burt Hooton (ingrown toenail) that forced Tommy Lasorda to use Valenzuela on Opening Day at Dodger Stadium against the Astros. Valenzuela was pitching batting practice the day before when summoned to Lasorda's office after Reuss injured himself while jogging in the parking lot.

Brito drove Valenzuela to the ballpark the next morning, but he didn't give a pep talk. Instead, Brito focused on giving a scouting report on Houston, noting that veterans Bob Watson and

Cesar Cedeno were high-ball hitters. "Fernando acted like he was going to pitch a game in the Mexican League," Brito said. "Nothing upset this guy." Brito nervously puffed on three cigars in the stands while watching his pitching prospect beat the Astros, 2–0, on a complete-game five-hitter.

Valenzuela became a sensation in both the United States and his native Mexico during the first two months of the season. He remains the only player in the Majors since Dave Ferris of the 1945 Boston Red Sox to win his first eight starts. By mid-May, Valenzuela was 8-0 with a 0.50 ERA and five shutouts.

"I don't think there's another player who created more baseball fans than Fernando," said Hall of Fame broadcaster Jaime Jarrín, who served as Valenzuela's interpreter during press conferences. "People here in the United States grew up with baseball; they played at school and knew the sport. But for three or four million Hispanics in Southern California, most of them grew up with soccer and were indifferent to baseball. But thanks to Fernando, they became baseball followers."

ABOVE After his pitching career, Fernando Valenzuela returned to the Dodgers as a broadcaster in 2003.

The Dodgers rushed the field after pitcher Jerry Reuss struck out Dave Roberts to end the 1981 NL Division Series against the Houston Astros.
OPPOSITE 1981 NLCS program featuring pitchers Burt Hooton, Jerry Reuss, Fernando Valenzuela and Bob Welch.

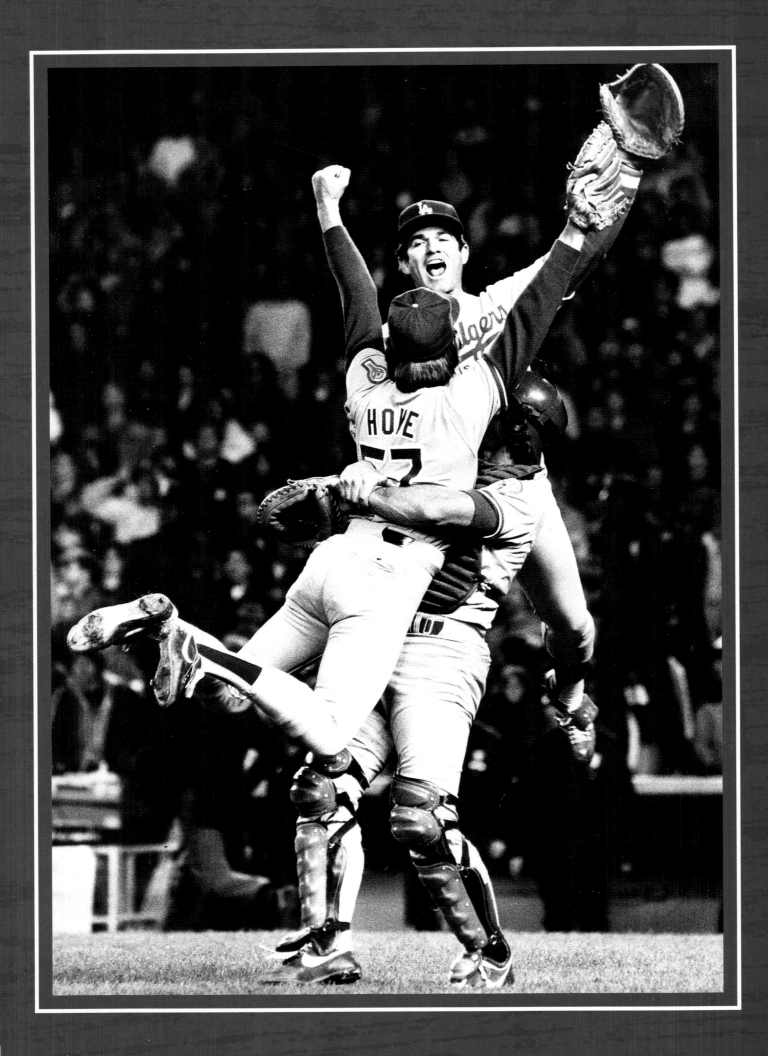

1981 World Series

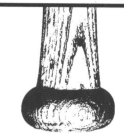

Sweeping three home games during the 1981 World Series gave the Dodgers a chance to preserve their string of unlikely comebacks during the postseason, following thrilling victories over the Houston Astros and the Montreal Expos.

But coming back against the New York Yankees represented redemption for the group of veterans who suffered through consecutive Fall Classic losses to Reggie Jackson and his pinstriped teammates in 1977 and 1978. It was Jackson who closed out the Yankees' victory in six games in 1977 with three home runs in consecutive at-bats against pitchers Burt Hooton, Elias Sosa and Charlie Hough. In 1978, the Dodgers were ahead two games to one in the Series and on top 3–1 in the sixth inning of Game 4 at Yankee Stadium. Shortstop Bill Russell knocked down a line drive by Lou Piniella and stepped on second base for the force on Jackson. On Russell's throw to first base, the ball hit Jackson, who appeared to stick his hip out. The Dodgers pleaded for interference and lost their composure when the call didn't go their way. The Yankees won the game in extra innings, and took the next two games.

So when the 1981 Dodgers lost the first two games at Yankee Stadium, there was guarded optimism in Los Angeles for Game 3, even with rookie sensation Fernando Valenzuela scheduled to oppose Yankees left-hander Dave Righetti. Ron Cey hit a three-run home run off Righetti in the first inning, but Valenzuela struggled early and Lasorda pondered whether to replace him when Valenzuela allowed four runs and six hits in the first three innings. Lasorda stayed with his ace, and the Dodgers escaped with a 5–4 victory.

The Dodgers tied the series with an 8–7 victory the following afternoon in a game in which the Yankees wasted leads of 4–0 and 6–3. Pinch-hitter Jay Johnstone's two-run home run off Ron Davis keyed a three-run sixth inning that tied the game at 6–6. The Dodgers scored twice in the seventh on a sacrifice fly by Steve Yeager and an RBI single by Davey Lopes. Jackson's home run in the eighth brought New York to within a run, but Steve Howe recorded the save in the ninth by retiring Willie Randolph on a flyout to center with runners on first and second.

The Game 5 matchup was a classic pitching battle between left-handers Jerry Reuss and Ron Guidry. Consecutive home runs by Pedro Guerrero and Yeager in the seventh inning spoiled Guidry's shutout bid and gave Reuss a 2–1 victory.

Back in New York for Game 6, Dodger players noticed it was strangely quiet during batting practice. The intimidation was gone, and the Dodgers won the Series with a 9–2 victory. It was only the second time the Dodgers had clinched a title at Yankee Stadium. The other was after Game 7 of the 1955 World Series, when Johnny Podres pitched a 2–0 shutout for Brooklyn's first and only championship.

OPPOSITE Reliever Steve Howe, catcher Steve Yeager and first baseman Steve Garvey celebrated the final out of 1981 World Series. **ABOVE** *(Left to right)* Tri-World Series MVPs Pedro Guerrero, Yeager and Ron Cey.

Rick Monday

BY ROY GLEASON

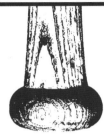

On April 25, 1976, when two protesters at Dodger Stadium tried to burn an American flag during a Dodgers-Cubs game, Chicago outfielder Rick Monday raced to the scene and grabbed the flag. Monday's heroics became a lasting image from the country's bicentennial celebration. Roy Gleason, a member of the Dodgers' 1963 championship team who later received a Purple Heart for his service in Vietnam, reflects on Monday's actions that afternoon.

Most of my family members served in the military during World War II, including my father, who was a Seabee in the Navy. I remember I was 3 years old in 1946 when my father walked into the house with a bumblebee logo on his uniform, which was the logo for the Seabees. They were the combat engineers that went in with the Marines. He was at Okinawa and Guadalcanal and the first invasion into Japan.

The day Rick saved the flag sticks out in my mind because it's important to me and I'm sure important to all other veterans, especially for those who have seen their colleagues make the ultimate sacrifice. In 1976, I was working for Don Drysdale at his bar from Tuesday through Saturday. But on Sundays, I worked at a place called the Godfather's in Tustin, which was located near Drysdale's place in Santa Ana. The Godfather's was like the bar on the television series *Cheers*, and I guess I was the original Woody character because the owner wanted me there because Sunday's crowd typically was a sports crowd. If the Dodgers were playing, the crowd at the bar was a mix of baseball fans, policemen and former members of the military. It was a raucous place. But I think I ended up working the shift for nothing because when Rick saved the flag, I bought everyone sitting at the bar a round of drinks.

When I think of the flag, I think about how it represents all our rights and freedoms as Americans. For someone to even think about burning a flag, it makes me upset. I'm glad it was Rick playing center field, and not me. He did the intelligent thing. I would've gone after both their heads. They probably would've dropped the match and the lighter fluid, and there would be a huge ball of flames out there. Whenever I see the photo or hear a replay of Vin Scully's radio broadcast, it brings tears to my eyes. It's really heartfelt, and he defended our country by protecting the American flag.

I never asked Rick about saving the flag. I know I thanked him. What he did was about the call of duty on a baseball field, because he could've just stood there. But he took action, and that's what a leader does. I know he spent time in the Marine Corps Reserves, so he knew about protocol and respect. Every time I see Rick, I picture Rick picking up the flag. That was a fantastic play on his part.

Roy Gleason *played for the Dodgers in 1963 before being drafted and serving his country in the Vietnam War. He was a sergeant in the United States Army where he earned a commendation for heroism and the Purple Heart.*

Rick Monday posed with James Roark, the *Los Angeles Herald-Examiner* photographer who captured the iconic image of Monday saving the American flag from being burned when Monday was at Dodger Stadium as a member of the Chicago Cubs on April 25, 1976.

Campy's Influence

BY MIKE SCIOSCIA

During his playing career with the Dodgers that spanned 1980 to 1992, Mike Scioscia built his reputation on defense—especially a fearless approach to blocking the plate. He was one of the quiet leaders of Dodger teams during his tenure, and from his earliest days in the Dodger organization, Scioscia forged a special bond with one of his catching forefathers, Roy Campanella, whose influence on young catchers was immediate and lasting, as evidenced by this first-person account:

Roy Campanella was one of the quietest men I've been around. But when he spoke, he spoke volumes.

He was very passionate—not only about the game of baseball, about winning, but about life. I met him when we were out on the field working out during Spring Training in Vero Beach in 1977.

As I got to know Roy over the years, I definitely considered him one of the biggest blessings that was ever brought into my life. I learned more about life than baseball, and he was an incredible human being who still has an impact on what I do on a day-to-day basis.

He was an eternal optimist. He was always upbeat. Roy never once talked about his accident or being in a wheelchair in all the years I knew him. I knew it was a tremendous ordeal for him just to get around and to get out to Spring Training and get out to the clubhouse and out to the stadium and work with the catchers. Never once did he say how tough it was. He was always ready, always wanted to help. I think the great pride he took in mentoring a young player like myself was something that had a huge impression on me about what my responsibilities are—not only in this game, but in being a role model that you might not perceive you are. His presence was very strong for such an incredibly humble man.

I was an 18-year-old kid at my first Spring Training on the first day of camp, and we finished up and went inside. I was obviously on cloud nine. It's your first day in big league camp, your first day on the field and you meet Roy Campanella. The next day before we started the workout, he was right next to me and he said, "Hey, you did great yesterday. You're going to be all right kid." That's all he said to me, and man, you talk about walking on air. What a feeling. Roy was a living legend.

He was from Nicetown—not far from where my father was born in Philadelphia. There was a connection there. We'd talk about Philadelphia, and he'd light up and smile. I knew how much he accomplished even before I was with the Dodgers. I knew how great a player he was and the unfortunate accident. But he was such a real person. He had this presence that I know I was attracted to. I absolutely thank God for being around him.

Mike Scioscia *played catcher on the Dodgers' World Series championship teams in 1981 and 1988. He was named manager of the Los Angeles Angels of Anaheim in 2000.*

PREVIOUS Steve Sax scored the first run of the Dodgers' 6–0 victory over the New York Mets in Game 7 of the 1988 NL Championship Series. **OPPOSITE ABOVE** Hall of Fame catcher Roy Campanella threw out the ceremonial first pitch to catcher Mike Scioscia as former pitcher Don Newcombe looked on prior to the 1988 NL Championship Series at Dodger Stadium. **ABOVE** Mike Scioscia's most memorable home run occurred in Game 4 of the 1988 NLCS at New York's Shea Stadium.

Orel Hershiser

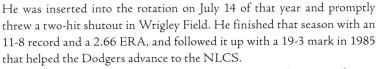

rel Leonard Hershiser IV—the name befits a banker, as do the boyish looks, red hair and gangly build that gave him the appearance of an adult version of Opie Taylor from The Andy Griffith Show.

Dodger Hall of Fame manager Tommy Lasorda sought to help the pitcher with a confidence boost. When Hershiser first reached the big leagues, Lasorda saw him pitch a few times before he called him in for a meeting.

"I said, 'You know something, you're the most negative pitcher I've ever seen,'" Lasorda said. "You know what your problem is? You're saying, 'I better not throw the ball there, or he's going to hit it,' instead of, 'I'm going to throw the ball there, and he's not going to hit it.' Now, that's the way you've got to think out there on that mound. And furthermore, I don't like your first name, Orel. From now on, your name is Bulldog."

Something clicked after Lasorda bestowed that nickname on Hershiser, who followed up an underwhelming 1983 September call-up by becoming a member of the Dodger bullpen in 1984.

He was inserted into the rotation on July 14 of that year and promptly threw a two-hit shutout in Wrigley Field. He finished that season with an 11-8 record and a 2.66 ERA, and followed it up with a 19-3 mark in 1985 that helped the Dodgers advance to the NLCS.

As great as that season was, it paled in comparison to the events of 1988. That year, Hall of Famer Don Drysdale joined the Dodger broadcasting team, and that reunion happened to occur on the 20th anniversary of his setting the Major League record with 58⅔ scoreless innings in 1968, a mark many thought to be untouchable.

Starting with the final four innings of a complete-game victory on August 30, Hershiser started a march toward that mark in earnest because the focus at that point was the pennant race. As he piled shutout on top of shutout, Hershiser's streak took on more attention, though Drysdale steered clear of the subject to keep from adding any extra pressure on Hershiser.

On the night of September 28, 1988, Hershiser took the mound after having strung together five straight shutouts and 49 consecutive zeroes. The Dodgers had clinched the NL West two days earlier, but there would be no rest for starting position players on this night.

The events of that evening worked out better than anyone could imagine. San Diego Padres pitcher Andy Hawkins kept the Dodgers scoreless through the first nine innings. Hershiser gave up just four hits and didn't allow a runner past first base until the 10th inning. Marvell Wynne struck out to open the 10th but reached first on Hershiser's wild pitch. Wynne advanced to second on a sacrifice and went to third on a groundout. After an intentional walk to Garry Templeton, Hershiser retired pinch-hitter Keith Moreland on a flyout to right fielder Jose Gonzalez.

With Hall of Famer Vin Scully calling the play-by-play in the broadcasting booth, Drysdale was stationed in the Dodger dugout in the ninth inning to conduct the postgame radio interview with a Dodger player. When Hershiser walked off the mound in the 10th inning, he was mobbed by his teammates. Then he reached Drysdale, who broke into a big smile and embraced Hershiser, telling him he was glad the record stayed in the Dodger family.

During his Cy Young Award season in 1988, right-hander Orel Hershiser went 23-8 with a 2.26 ERA and a string of 59 consecutive scoreless innings.

"I really and truly did not want to break the record," Hershiser said in that dugout interview with Drysdale. "Out of respect to the man sitting next to me, I feel I should've stopped at two-thirds. I wanted to just put the ball down, but the guys next to me in the dugout convinced me to go for it."

Drysdale replied, "If I had known that, I would've been down there kicking you by the seat of your pants."

The streak also clinched the National League Cy Young Award for Hershiser, who went 23-8 with a 2.26 ERA during the regular season.

"When he went through that streak of 59 innings," reminisced Kirk Gibson, Hershiser's teammate and the National League MVP that year, "I remember I would be out in left field, and I'm not kidding—it seemed like the first four or five innings, you could just take your glove off, because if anything was going to come to you, it was just lame. He just dominated. He had such control over all his pitches. Tommy nicknamed him the Bulldog, and he was. He was a bulldog. He had it all working. It was a huge asset for our team to know that when Orel went to the mound like that, that, really, we were going to win."

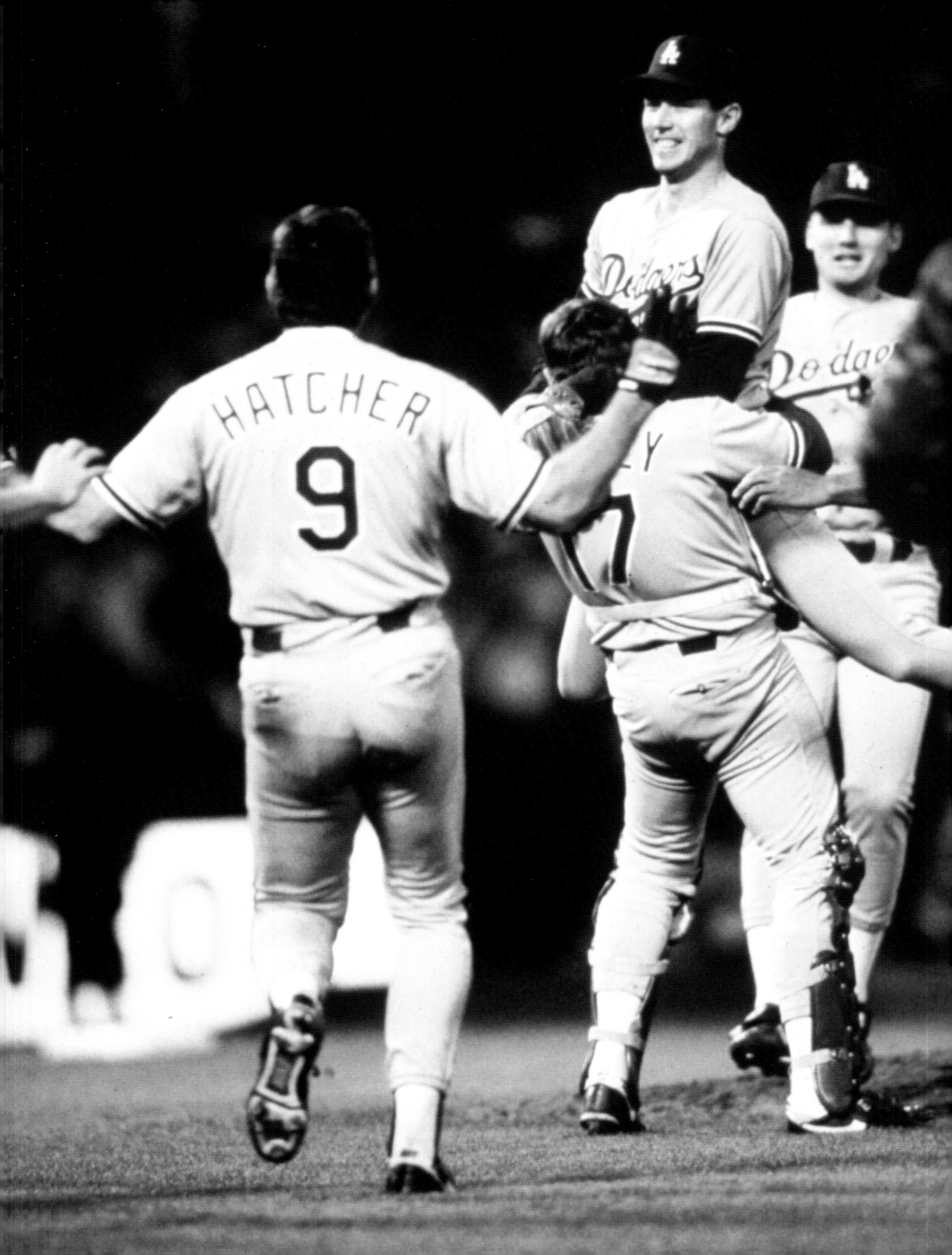
HATCHER
9
Dodgers
Dodgers

1988 World Series

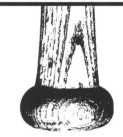

The shortest World Series in history lasted only nine innings in 1988. At least that's what one might believe after hearing the Dodgers declare in retrospect that the Fall Classic was over after Kirk Gibson's dramatic home run against the Oakland Athletics.

Due to knee and hamstring injuries, Gibson—the NL Most Valuable Player in 1988 and the Dodgers' inspirational leader—wasn't able to start Game 1 in Los Angeles. As the Dodgers trailed 4–3 in the ninth inning, Gibson hobbled to the plate with two outs and Mike Davis on first base. Davis eventually stole second and, on a tip from Dodger scout Mel Didier and with a full-count pitch, Gibson looked for a backdoor slider from Dennis Eckersley. Swinging off his front foot, Gibson somehow pulled the ball into the Right Field Pavilion. He hobbled around the bases, and the Dodgers celebrated a 5–4 victory.

But Gibson wouldn't play again in the Series, so it was still up to his teammates to finish the job. Game 2 was crucial for the Dodgers if they wanted to retain the momentum, and because they knew the next three games would be in Oakland. A three-run home run by Dodger Mike Marshall off Storm Davis keyed a five-run outburst in the third inning. Orel Hershiser scattered three hits en route to a complete-game 6–0 victory, and at the plate, he became the first pitcher to have three hits in a World Series game since 1924.

In Game 3, Dodger starter John Tudor was out by the second inning due to tightness in his shoulder. Former Dodger pitcher Bob Welch and three Oakland relievers held the Dodgers to one run on eight hits, and Mark McGwire's walk-off home run in the bottom of the ninth inning off reliever Jay Howell gave Oakland a 2–1 victory.

Prior to the Fall Classic, NBC broadcaster Bob Costas said the 1988 Dodgers had perhaps the weakest lineup in World Series history. Dodger manager Tommy Lasorda used Costas' comments to motivate his club, but the offense still had to manufacture runs, especially in the 4–3 victory in Game 4. The Dodgers scored in the first inning when Steve Sax walked, went to third on Mickey Hatcher's single and scored on catcher Ron Hassey's passed ball. Hatcher scored the second run on a groundout by John Shelby. The Dodgers scored their third run in the third when Franklin Stubbs doubled and came home on a throwing error by shortstop Walt Weiss.

Hershiser wrapped up the Series with a 5–2 victory in Game 5. Hatcher, subbing for Gibson in left field, hit a two-run homer in the first inning. It was the second Series home run for Hatcher, who had just one homer during the regular season in 191 at-bats. Mike Davis, who batted .196 during the regular season, hit a two-run home run in the fourth. Former World Series MVP Rick Dempsey, filling in for injured catcher Mike Scioscia, hit an RBI double in the sixth.

PREVIOUS Kirk Gibson hugged manager Tommy Lasorda at home plate after his home run in Game 1 of the 1988 World Series. Making sure Gibson touched the plate was umpire Doug Harvey. **OPPOSITE** After the Dodgers clinched the 1988 World Series with a 5–2 victory in Game 5 at Oakland, pitcher Orel Hershiser was lifted into the air by catcher Rick Dempsey as Mickey Hatcher and Jeff Hamilton rushed the scene. **ABOVE** The team was saluted by President Ronald Reagan at the White House.

The 1990s

Homegrown Talent

BY ERIC KARROS

I was aware of the Dodgers at age 4 or 5. My dad was a huge Dodger fan growing up in Utica, New York. He was born in Brooklyn, and he used to listen to all the Dodger games on the radio. Ironically, after he graduated from Yale and went into the service with the Marines, he wanted to get stationed at Camp Pendleton. The reason? The Dodgers had moved to Los Angeles.

He ended up marrying my mom, and for their honeymoon, they spent the weekend watching Sandy Koufax and Don Drysdale pitch at Dodger Stadium. So already, there's quite a bit of Dodger stuff going on. We used to go up as a family and watch the Dodgers-Reds series in the 1970s. I'll never forget one of my early trips to the stadium. In those days, the players went into the stands and signed autographs. I bought a black-and-white photo pack and still have signed photos from people like Davey Lopes, Red Adams, Bill Russell and Steve Garvey. So that was my introduction to the Dodgers.

Our family lived in San Diego, and every night, my dad listened to a little transistor radio. The only place you could get good reception was in his office, and you had to have the radio on a certain part of his desk. Every night, it was the same routine: Vin Scully and the Dodger games. Ironically, growing up, I was a fan of Pete Rose and the Cincinnati Reds. My brother was a huge Steve Garvey fan, and he loved the Dodgers. I don't know if I rooted for the Reds to spite everyone.

I ended up getting drafted by the Dodgers out of UCLA in 1988. I didn't realize at the time what it meant for my dad for his son to get drafted by the Dodgers,

let alone being able to play for the ballclub. But now, as a dad, I realize it was the best gift I could've given him. The Dodger tradition, the Dodger play—I was inundated with it growing up. One of the first things I did in Spring Training was bring a baseball my dad had caught as a kid when Don Newcombe hit a home run off Sal Maglie. I got it signed by Newk.

I owe a lot to Fred Claire, the general manager, and Tommy Lasorda for giving me an opportunity as a rookie in 1992. That season, although it was rewarding for me as an individual, was a long year. But at that stage, I was just trying to survive. Every day was exciting, because I was in the big leagues. The first half of the season, I'm not playing that much, so I'm not thinking about Rookie of the Year. In the second half, Tommy had me hitting third or fourth, and he would have guys bunting in the first inning to get guys in scoring position for me. So Tommy played a huge role in that.

Right around that time of the early 1990s, the farm system was stacked. I got to know Mike Piazza well in the instructional league, and then he came up to the Dodgers at the end of 1992. We lived together for a number of years. He had one of the best rookie seasons in

the history of the game in 1993. And then Raul Mondesi in 1994, Hideo Nomo in 1995, Todd Hollandsworth in 1996—it just seemed like one guy after another.

The Nomo experience was something. Although there had been a Japanese player in the 1960s—a left-handed pitcher for the San Francisco Giants named Masanori Murakami—nobody had exploded onto the scene like Nomo. For what he did, to provide opportunities for future Japanese players, he had the weight of everything on his shoulders. Just to be around and watch him handle

those things, he couldn't go anywhere without a horde of reporters around him. Hollandsworth finished it up, and the Dodgers had five consecutive Rookies of the Year.

That was a time we were a good, young team. We could never get over the top, but there were a lot of fun and memorable times. You talk about the Dodgers and being able to develop their own—it was just like the time from 1979 to 1982, when the Dodgers had four consecutive Rookies of the Year with Rick Sutcliffe, Steve Howe, Fernando Valenzuela and Steve Sax.

During the 1996 season, Tommy Lasorda suffered a heart attack in June, but we thought he was coming back after a rest. But Tommy stepping down instead and retiring—I never thought I'd see that. Bill Russell had been around as a longtime coach, and he took over as manager. It was a completely different environment going from Tommy, being boisterous and loud, to Billy, who was different.

I will say the 1997 team was the best of any team we had in the decade. That was the year we did not make the playoffs, and the Florida Marlins ended up winning the World Series. But two things I'll always remember around that time were Billy taking over the

Dodgers and Peter O'Malley selling the club. Before Mr. O'Malley made the announcement to the public, he had a conference call, and there were many of the players on the line. He says he's made a family decision to sell the club. I'm thinking, "You've got to be kidding me. There's no way." At the end of the call, I said, "Mr. O'Malley, I just wanted to thank you for the opportunity, and I think I'm speaking on behalf of the other players on the phone."

A lot of times, you think the grass is greener on the other side. But the O'Malley era was unique because of the way we were treated. Whether you were a minor leaguer or a big leaguer, you were treated as a Dodger. If you were working in the front office in Los Angeles, working somewhere at Dodgertown or at any of the minor league affiliates, you were part of the Dodger family. I remember as a Dodger minor leaguer, I'm eating in the same place—the same food—as Orel Hershiser and Kirk Gibson and Tommy Lasorda. That just wasn't the case in any other organization. I was fortunate to play under the O'Malley ownership.

I had a chance during my time with the Dodgers to hit 270 home runs, which surpassed the previous Los Angeles record of 228 home runs set by Ron Cey. It's a nice accomplishment for me personally, looking at the guys who have gone through the organization and have played at Dodger Stadium. Matt Kemp, in 2011, was the first L.A. Dodger to ever outright lead the league in home runs. And Dodger Stadium is not an easy place to hit home runs. When you talk about my home runs, people might ask, "Did you get to 300?" Well, no, but I think, playing in that ballpark, it was still a pretty decent accomplishment. I tried to be consistent and a guy you could count on every year.

But more than anything, it was an honor just playing for the Dodgers and being discussed in the same breath as a lot of other players who have worn a Brooklyn or Los Angeles uniform. Again, I grew up knowing about Gil Hodges and Duke Snider and Carl Furillo and Sandy Amoros. I knew all of that. And being able to grow up in the organization and see Johnny Podres and Sandy Koufax, and see all these guys who I heard stories about when I was a kid, and how they impacted my father, that experience supersedes any experience that I had on the field, whether it was getting a hit here or there, or hitting a home run, or getting to the playoffs. I appreciate that more as I've grown older and gotten further removed from the game. But the greatest gift was just having an opportunity to experience something so few have ever had.

Eric Karros played for the Dodgers from 1991 to 2002. He was named the 1992 National League Rookie of the Year and earned a Silver Slugger Award in 1995.

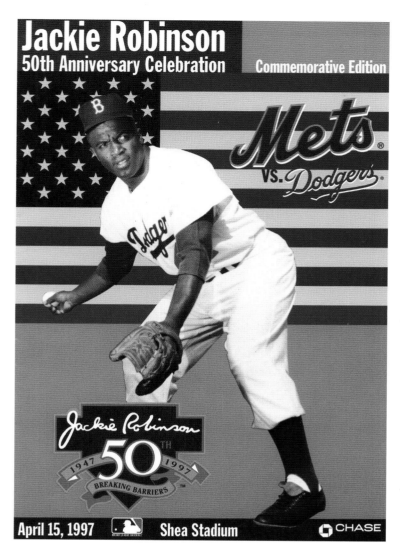

OPPOSITE TOP *(Left to right)* Carl Erskine, Don Drysdale, Duke Snider and Reggie Smith posed during a 100th Anniversary luncheon prior to the 1990 season. **OPPOSITE BOTTOM** Relief pitcher Jim Gott, *right,* was a third-degree black belt in the Hapkido martial arts during his Dodger career from 1990 to 1994. **ABOVE** On the 50th anniversary of his Brooklyn Dodger debut in 1947, Jackie Robinson's uniform No. 42 was retired by all Major League teams. **BELOW** Dodger Spanish language broadcaster Jaime Jarrín, *left,* received his Hall of Fame certificate from Ralph Kiner during induction ceremonies at Cooperstown in 1998.

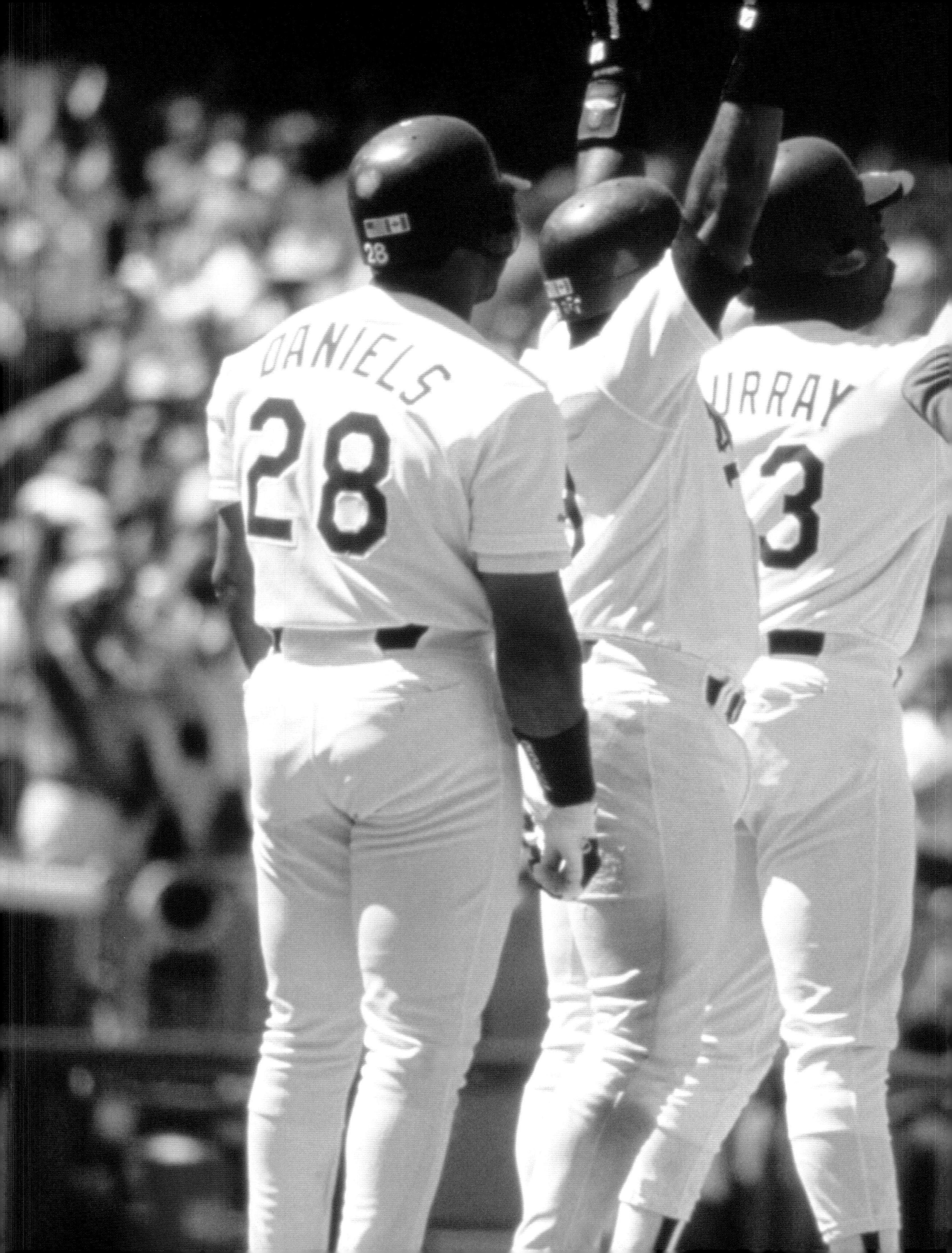
DANIELS
28

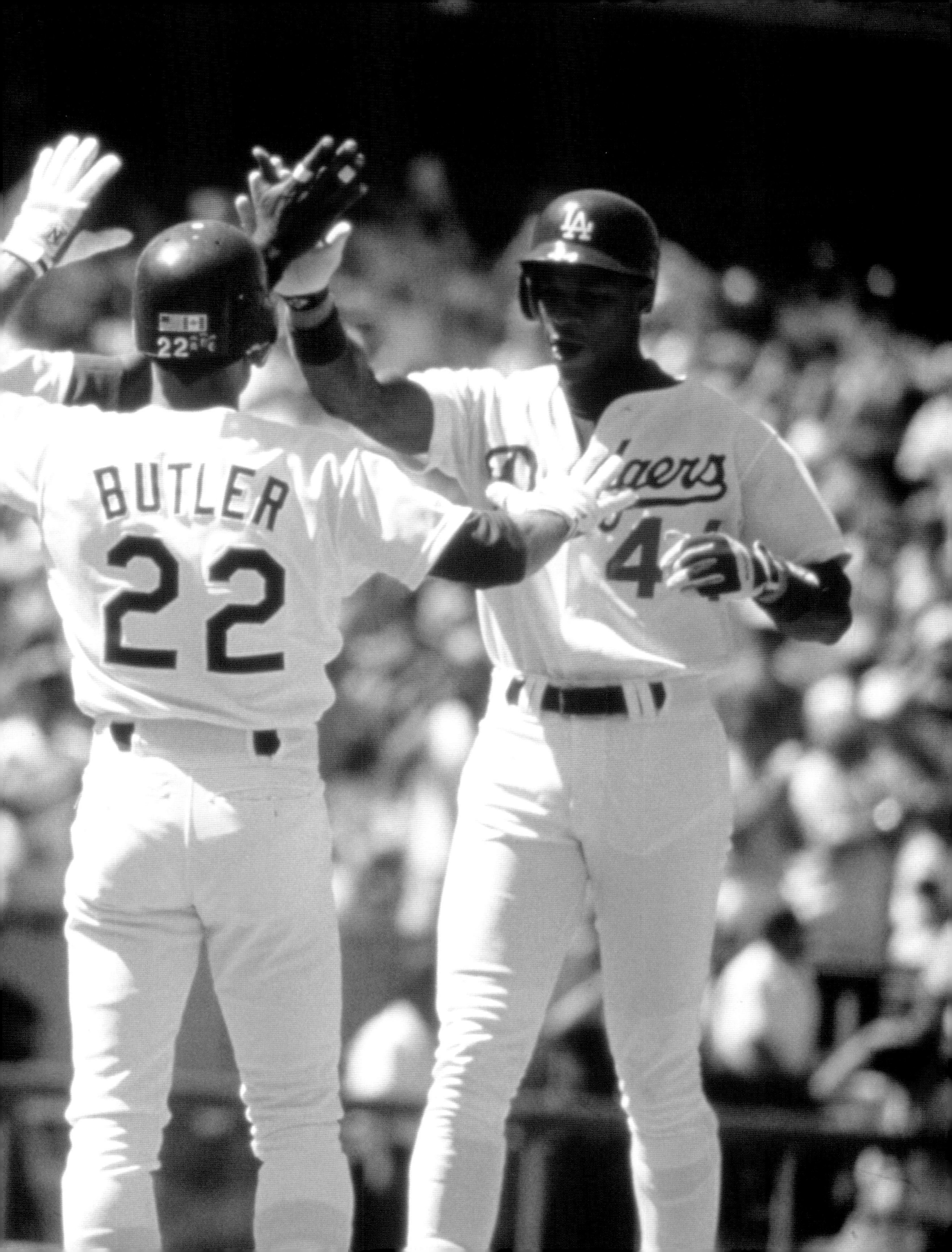
BUTLER
22

Volume 4, Number 6

Eddie Murray: Consistent Excellence

Includes California State sales tax $2.25

MAGAZINE

Dodgers

AND SCORECARD

STANDING
TALL

RAMON

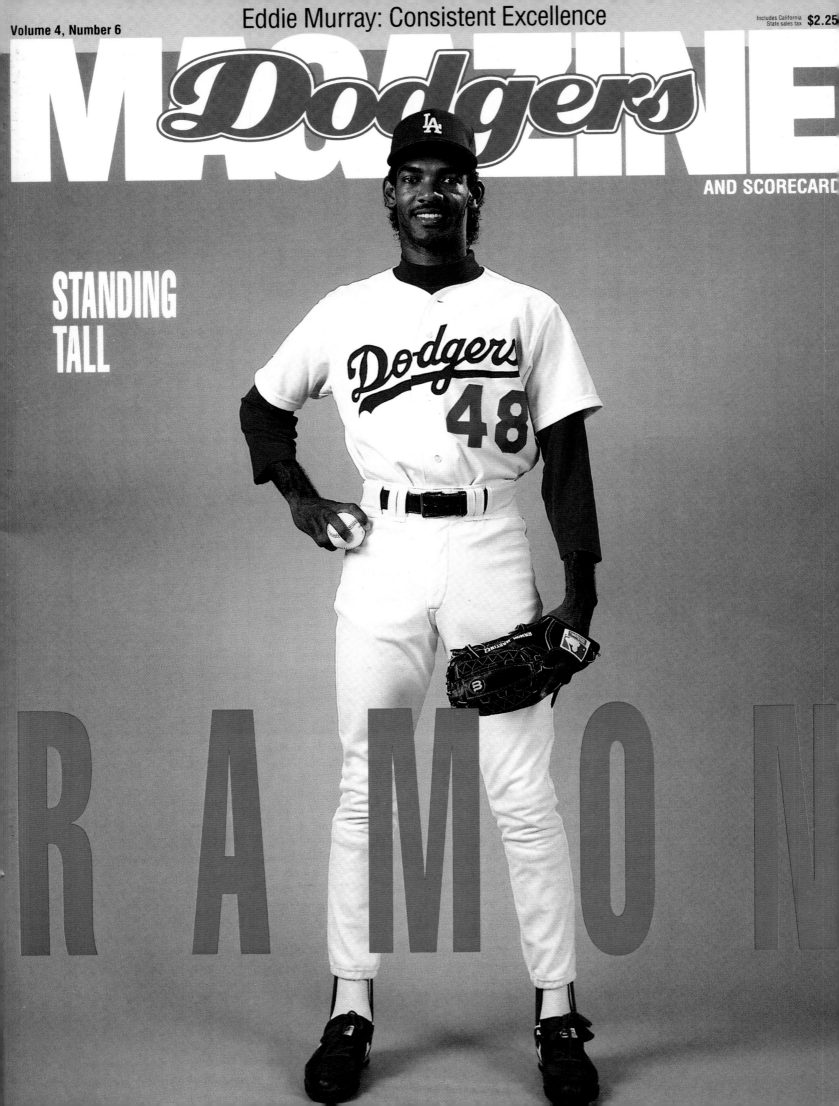

Ramon Martinez

T here was a time when Ramon Martinez was the most famous pitcher in his family. Before younger brother Pedro came along and won three Cy Young Awards, Ramon burst on the scene in Southern California as a 20-game winner at age 22 in 1990. Martinez was the youngest Dodger to win 20 games since Brooklyn's Ralph Branca at age 21 in 1947. He finished second in the Cy Young voting to Pittsburgh Pirate Doug Drabek. "Everybody in the Dominican Republic prays for Ramon and roots for him," Dodger coach Manny Mota said in 1991. "They know they might be seeing in Ramon a future Hall of Famer, God willing."

Because Martinez was so young, it was natural to compare his potential with that of Hall of Fame pitcher Sandy Koufax. Martinez already had made great progress after the Dodgers signed him as a free agent in 1984. There was a time when Martinez weighed 140 pounds, so the Dodgers arranged for an unlimited tab at a cafeteria in his native Dominican Republic in hopes he would acquire enough bulk to cover his lightning-rod physique. Martinez would win 123 games with the Dodgers from 1988 to 1998, but never again did he reach his previous level of dominance.

The most memorable game of his career occurred on June 4, 1990 against the Atlanta Braves at Dodger Stadium. During a 6–0 victory, Martinez tied Koufax's single-game team mark of 18 strikeouts. It could have been more, because Martinez still had four outs remaining when he fanned No. 18, Jeff Blauser, for the second out of the eighth inning. Veteran Mickey Hatcher, making a rare start at first base, was loudly booed when making two outstanding plays on grounders, one to end the eighth inning and the other for the second out of the ninth. Hatcher's defense helped preserve Martinez's shutout but also cost him a chance at the Major League record of 20 strikeouts.

"When I started playing catch in the bullpen, I felt like it was going to be my night," said Martinez, who entered the game with a 5-3 record and a 3.63 ERA. "I think that was the turning point for my confidence. It was like throwing a no-hitter. I felt like a different guy after the game. I felt like I was a hero and I could win a lot of ballgames."

Martinez appeared on pace to win 20 again in 1991, but he was struck on the elbow by a Jack Howell line drive while earning his 15th victory on August 20. He insisted he was fine but went 2-5 in his final eight starts, and the Dodgers lost the NL West to Atlanta by one game.

Martinez pitched a no-hitter against the Florida Marlins on July 14, 1995 at Dodger Stadium. He and Koufax are the only pitchers in Dodger history to pitch at least one no-hitter and strike out 18 batters in a game.

PREVIOUS Darryl Strawberry arrived at home plate after his grand slam against the San Diego Padres at Dodger Stadium on August 21, 1991. Greeting Strawberry are *(left to right)* Kal Daniels, Lenny Harris, Eddie Murray and Brett Butler. **OPPOSITE** Cover of 1991 *Dodgers Magazine*. **ABOVE** Ramon Martinez held the baseball from his no-hitter against Florida at Dodger Stadium on July 14, 1995.

Kevin Gross pitched his only career no-hitter against the
San Francisco Giants at Dodger Stadium on August 17, 1992.

Mike Piazza

O pening Day 1993 represented a baseball homecoming for Dodger manager Tommy Lasorda when his team was chosen to play in the Florida Marlins' debut game. The opposing pitcher who defeated Orel Hershiser and the Dodgers that afternoon was 45-year-old Charlie Hough, whose baseball career was saved by Lasorda as a minor leaguer in 1970 when the manager suggested that the struggling pitcher learn how to throw the knuckleball.

In the 1993 Los Angeles lineup was rookie catcher Mike Piazza, the son of Lasorda's longtime friend Vince Piazza. When the Dodgers played in Piazza's hometown of Philadelphia, Mike often visited the clubhouse and served as the team's batboy. It was Lasorda who originally helped Piazza, coming out of Miami-Dade Community College, become a 62nd-round draft choice in 1988. Lasorda made another "suggestion," and Piazza learned to catch, even flying to the team's camp in the Dominican Republic for additional workouts.

Although Piazza's rising stock in the minor leagues warranted a chance with Los Angeles, Lasorda didn't want to put any extra pressure on Piazza as the replacement for veteran Mike

Scioscia. Yet Piazza's talent was undeniable, making Lasorda's decision easy to name him the first rookie catcher to start on Opening Day in Los Angeles history.

Piazza would enjoy the most prolific rookie season in Los Angeles history. He batted .318 with 35 home runs and 112 RBI. The home runs established a Los Angeles Dodger single-season record, and the RBI total established a Dodger rookie record. Both his home run and RBI totals rank third all-time among NL rookies.

On the final day of the season, the Dodgers played host to the San Francisco Giants on October 3, the anniversary of two famous dates in the rivalry between the two franchises. It was on October 3, 1951 when Bobby Thomson of the New York Giants beat the Brooklyn Dodgers with a ninth-inning home run in the third and deciding playoff game at the Polo Grounds. By 1962, both teams had relocated to the West Coast, but the script remained the same that year as the Giants staged a ninth-inning comeback at Dodger Stadium in the decisive playoff game.

In 1993, the Giants had a 103-58 record after 161 games but still needed a victory on the final day to force a one-game playoff against the Atlanta Braves in the NL West. Piazza ruined San Francisco's plans with two home runs in a 12–1 victory.

In 726 games with Los Angeles, Piazza compiled a .331 average with 177 home runs and 563 RBI. In his final full season with the Dodgers in 1997, Piazza hit .362 with 40 home runs and 124 RBI, finishing second in the NL MVP balloting. He holds the all-time record for most home runs by a catcher (396) and finished with 427 home runs during his 16-year career.

In 726 games with Los Angeles, Mike Piazza batted .331 with 177 home runs and 563 RBI.

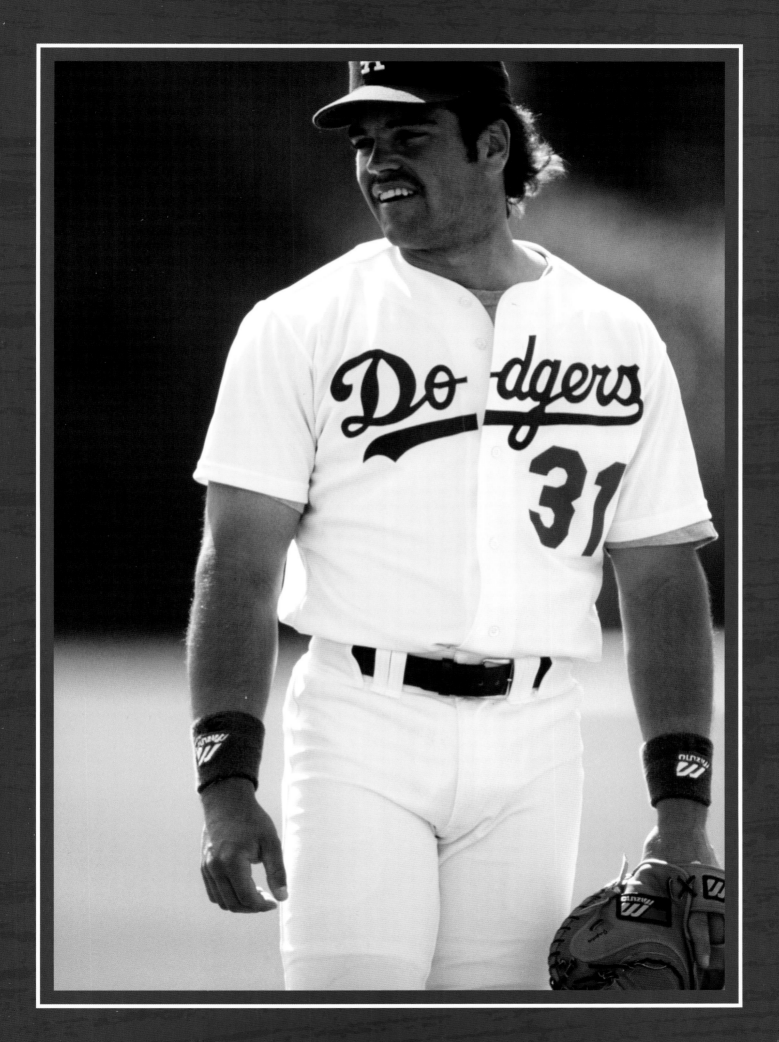

Taiwan

When the Dodgers reached out to Taiwan in the '90s, it was with the hope that they could eventually tap the national talent that had yielded more than half the Little League World Series championship teams during the previous two decades. Thus, after the 1993 season—as part of the Friendship Baseball Series, which also included a stop in Japan—the Dodgers became the first Major League Baseball team to play in Taiwan.

The Dodgers played three games against the Chinese Professional League All-Stars. In 1996, the Dodgers established a working agreement with the Sinon Bulls of the Chinese Professional Baseball League. The Bulls became the first team from Taiwan to train in Latin America when they visited the Dodgers' Campo Las Palmas baseball academy in 1997.

This outreach quickly produced results.

Pitcher Hong Chih-Kuo, in 1999, became the first Taiwanese high school baseball player to sign a professional contract. Kuo, who made his Major League debut in 2005 for the Dodgers, five years later established the team record for the lowest earned run average (1.20) for a pitcher with at least 50 innings.

In November 2002, the Dodgers became the first MLB organization with two Taiwanese players—Kuo and outfielder Chin-Feng Chen—on the 40-man roster. On September 9, 2002, Chen became the first Taiwanese player in the Majors. (Kuo became the fourth in 2005.) On January 29, 2007, the Dodgers signed right-handed pitcher Chin-hui Tsao to a one-year contract, giving them three out of the four Taiwanese-born players to ever appear in a Major League game. In 2007, infielder Chin-lung Hu made it four out of five.

In 2010, the Dodgers returned to Taiwan for three scheduled games against a team from the Chinese Professional Baseball League, and Kuo and Hu participated in a youth-baseball clinic with Dodger coaches and local coaches at the Taipei Municipal Tienmu Stadium. Manager Joe Torre hosted a baseball leadership clinic for the prime minister and about 50 Taiwanese coaches and officials. "There's not a magical formula," Torre told the attendees. "But don't forget, they all are people. I try to make every player feel important. In a long season, you will need every player to contribute—whether it's small or large. There's no such thing as an insignificant contribution." At the ballpark, Taiwanese players walked over to the Dodger dugout and asked an official if they would get Torre's autograph on baseballs. One even had a copy of Torre's book, translated into Chinese.

The Saturday night game was delayed by rain and eventually canceled because of the weather. Sensing that the game might not be played, the players from the Dodger and Taiwanese teams began throwing signed baseballs into the grandstands, followed by hats and any other souvenirs that could be found.

The final game was staged at the 20,000-seat Kaohsiung County Stadium, where Hu recorded three hits in an 11–1 victory. The postgame scene included Kuo and Hu addressing the crowd in Chinese and the players again throwing baseballs into an appreciative and excited crowd. "They are just genuine fans," Torre said. "That's pretty cool. That's the reason for the team to come to Taiwan. You don't realize how far we reach."

OPPOSITE The Dodgers visited Taiwan on two occasions in 1993 and 2010.

A fixture behind home plate with his radar gun and Panama hat when Dodger Stadium had "dugout level" seats through the 1999 season, Dodger scout Mike Brito is best known for signing pitcher Fernando Valenzuela in 1979.

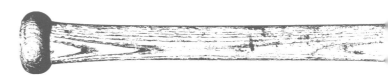

Japan

Beyond the center field parking lot at Dodger Stadium, nestled on the hillside, is a Japanese garden, which might seem out of the ordinary for a Major League ballpark. But the Dodgers' relationship with Japan began when the franchise was in Brooklyn and continued on the West Coast, long before Los Angeles signed pitcher Hideo Nomo in 1995.

The centerpiece of the garden is a 10-foot-tall stone lantern weighing nearly 4,000 pounds. When the stadium opened with a civic luncheon on April 9, 1962, one of the guests for the first game was the dean of Japanese sportswriters, Sotaro Suzuki, who had served as an interpreter during the Dodgers' first goodwill trip to Japan in 1956. Suzuki also traveled in 1957 to the Dodgers' training camp in Vero Beach, Florida with three members of the Tokyo Giants.

Upon returning to Japan in 1962, Suzuki decided to give Walter O'Malley and the Dodgers an *ishi-doro* (stone lantern), which was built by the Shimizugumi Stone Works Company, a famous stone-carving house in Aichi Prefecture. Shipped in six pieces, the lantern arrived in

the winter of 1965. The inscription on the back of the lantern base reads, "To commemorate the opening of Dodger Stadium on April 9, 1962—Donated by Sotaro and Toku Suzuki, Guests."

The Dodgers made three postseason tours of Japan in 1956, 1966 and 1993, which led to return visits by the Tokyo Giants during Spring Training on five occasions between 1961 and 1980.

In 1964 and 1965, the Dodgers conducted coaching clinics in Japan. Scouting Director Al Campanis visited Kawasaki to conduct the 1964 clinic for the Taiyo Whales, and scouts Tommy Lasorda and Kenny Myers conducted the 1965 clinic in Tokyo and Miyazaki for the Tokyo Giants. Lasorda became manager of the Dodgers in September 1976 and in 1979 managed the National League All-Star team during a

seven-game series in Japan. By 2000, Lasorda had retired as manager, but as team vice president, he visited the Osaka Kintetsu Buffaloes 15 times over a three-year period as part of the team's Friendship Agreement with the Buffaloes to help with baseball instruction and coaching.

In December 2008, Lasorda was presented with the Order of the Rising Sun Award by the consul general of Japan, Junichi Ihara, for his contributions to Japanese baseball. Ike Ikuhara, a member of the Dodger front office from 1965 until his passing in 1993, became a liaison for the Dodgers during the Tokyo Giants visits, and he represented Team President Peter O'Malley on many international trips. (Ikuhara was named to the Japan Baseball Hall of Fame in Tokyo in 2002.) Each year, the Dodgers host interns from Waseda University, Ikuhara's alma mater, for several weeks and teach them about baseball and American culture.

ABOVE Ron Fairly posed with Tokyo Giants stars Sadaharu Oh, *center*, and Shigeo Nagashima, *right*, during Spring Training at Vero Beach in 1967. **OPPOSITE** The sketch on the 1956 Japan tour program featured shortstop Pee Wee Reese.

週刊読売 臨時増刊

第二九二号週刊読売第十五巻第四十五号　昭和三十一年十月二十日発行（臨時増刊）

ドジャースの全容

30円

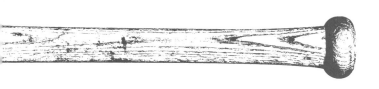

Hideo Nomo

Before Hideo Nomo in 1995, the story line of a Japanese player traveling to the United States for a Major League career was strictly material for a Hollywood movie studio. But his sensational debut not only garnered National League Rookie of the Year honors but also opened the door for other Japanese stars.

Superstars like Ichiro Suzuki and Hideki Matsui have become commonplace among the MLB rosters, so it's important to remember the pressure Nomo faced when he joined the Dodgers. After a successful five-year career with the Osaka Kintetsu Buffaloes, the right-hander "retired" from Japanese baseball following the 1994 season and shopped his services to the Majors, a bold and almost unprecedented move for someone of Nomo's generation.

Pitcher Masanori Murakami (San Francisco Giants, 1964–65) was the only other Japanese player to have appeared in the Major Leagues up to that time; he returned to his native country partly because of political pressure. Nomo had reached the 1,000-strikeout plateau faster than any other pitcher in the history of Japanese professional baseball. Although tendinitis limited him to just 17 starts in 1994, several MLB teams courted Nomo after watching a two-minute videotape of his career highlights.

"He just had that presence about him, the presence of a winner," said Fred Claire, the Dodger general manager from 1987 to 1998. "Here's a guy who had everything. He put everything on the table— fame, fortune and all the conveniences anyone would ever want. What he was saying was, 'I'm willing to risk everything just to go out there against the best.' Perhaps the most memorable thing he said to me is, 'I haven't proven anything yet. I've done nothing.' That impressed me. That impressed me a lot."

In 28 regular-season starts, Nomo went 13-6 with a 2.54 ERA and 236 strikeouts in 191⅓ innings. Nomo, the first Japanese player selected to an All-Star team, led the Dodgers with three shutouts. He became only the third Dodger rookie to lead the NL in strikeouts, joining Brooklyn's Dazzy Vance (1922) and Fernando Valenzuela (1981). Nomo struck out 13 or more batters five times in 1995 and fanned 10 or more batters 11 times. (Sandy Koufax is the only other Dodger pitcher to record 10 or more strikeouts in a game eight times.) On June 14, Nomo struck out 16 Pittsburgh Pirates to set a single-game Dodger rookie record, surpassing the 15 strikeouts by Brooklyn's Karl Spooner in 1954.

Nomo had two stints with the Dodgers (1995–1998, 2002–2004) and pitched a no-hitter at Colorado's Coors Field in 1996. When he threw a no-hitter for the Boston Red Sox in 2001, Nomo became the fourth pitcher in MLB history with no-nos in each league, following Cy Young, Jim Bunning and Nolan Ryan (later to be joined by Randy Johnson).

Hideo Nomo made his Major League debut with five scoreless innings against the San Francisco Giants on May 2, 1995 at San Francisco.

CHAPTER

8

The 2000s and Beyond

New Heroes

BY SHAWN GREEN

Having spent my grade school years in San Jose, California near San Francisco, I was aware of the rivalry between the Giants and the Dodgers. I wasn't dedicated to any particular team; instead, I was a fan of the game and rooted for certain players. Our family moved to Southern California when I was 12, and my biggest memory of Dodger Stadium at that time was being there for Game 1 of the 1988 World Series. We had seats way up top in right field—directly above the grass where I yearned to stand someday.

I was playing on a scout team as a sophomore in high school. At the game, one of the scouts asked if anyone wanted to buy his World Series tickets, because he couldn't go. We bought them, and on the way to the stadium, we ran by a sporting goods store and grabbed a sweat suit for me to wear in lieu of my dirty uniform. I'm ashamed to say that we were guilty of leaving right before Kirk Gibson hit the home run, and, like many others, my parents and I ran back into the stadium to see why the crowd had erupted so intensely.

Coming back to Dodger Stadium as a player in 2000 was a dream come true. But the first year did feel a bit strange. Back in Toronto, my baseball world and my California home were two separate places. Then, all of a sudden, I found myself working in the same place where I was used to being off during the winter. I associated Toronto with playing baseball, because that was the only reason I was there. Prior to my trade to the Dodgers, on the other hand, Southern California represented everything *but* baseball to me.

Coming to Dodger Stadium to play was awesome. I went from Toronto, which was very supportive of the Blue Jays but still a hockey town, to Los Angeles. (Some people might say L.A. is a basketball town because of the Lakers, but I think L.A. has always been the Dodgers' town.) I also went from playing on AstroTurf in a futuristic stadium to playing on the most well-manicured grass in the big leagues, inside one of the older, most historic stadiums in the game.

Needless to say, I was right where I wanted to be.

I came over at a time when the team was trying to be the Yankees of the West, though that wasn't working too well. There were high-priced superstars, but there wasn't much chemistry. Every year, though, the environment improved. Some of the guys from the farm system started to have a big impact, like Paul Lo Duca, who got his chance in 2001, and Eric Gagné, who really got going in 2002. Other homegrown guys, such as Alex Cora, were contributing as well. The Dodgers have a rich history of developing great talent, and once the organization went back to putting faith in the farm system, everything started coming together. We became more cohesive, and a lot of the bigger egos had moved on to other organizations.

Eric Gagné's streak of 84 consecutive saves was probably the most amazing feat I saw in my 14 years in the Major Leagues. To do what he did was one thing. But the way he did it was that much more impressive. Of the 84 saves,

ABOVE FROM LEFT The Dodgers celebrated the 50th anniversary of the 1955 championship team, which included *(left to right)* Carl Erskine, Johnny Podres and Sandy Koufax; Eric Gagné converted all 55 of his save opportunities during his Cy Young Award season in 2003; Shawn Green connected on his Major League record-tying fourth home run on May 23, 2002 in Milwaukee.

maybe three or four games were nail-biters. He was so dominant. On the field, we all talked about how we would get chills when he came into the game—they blared Guns N' Roses, his cartoon-face logo was on every scoreboard and the whole stadium was rocking. Fans who used to leave in the seventh or eighth inning were hanging around for the ninth because he was the highlight of the show. Gagné fed on that persona he had created: the way he would approach the mound, the way his shirt came untucked, the sweat on his hat, the glasses. It was a different experience from anything I'd ever seen in baseball.

My last year as a Dodger was 2004, and it was by far the wildest. We were finally leading the division for most of the season, and then the trading deadline arrived at the end of July. We were expecting to acquire a few helping hands, but instead a quarter of our team was traded away—key guys like Lo Duca, Guillermo Mota, Dave Roberts and Juan Encarnacion. For several days, our clubhouse atmosphere was in disarray. We were scratching and clawing in an attempt to get to the finish line for the first time in years. By September, the race got tighter and the Giants were really on us. We were struggling offensively the last week. After losing the opening game of the series against them, the final weekend of the regular season, we were ahead by only two games, with two remaining. We knew that if we didn't win on Saturday, we were going to be in trouble. Their ace, Jason Schmidt, was slated to pitch on Sunday, and they won the coin flip—securing them the home-field advantage for the potential tiebreaker on Monday.

Our starting pitching was sort of in a shambles because some guys were hurt. Thus, for this crucial Saturday game, we had to rely on a spot start by reliever Elmer Dessens,

followed by anyone and everyone in our bullpen. We had been struggling to score runs in that last week, and this Saturday game was no different. The Giants were ahead 3–0 entering the bottom of the ninth inning. I led off the inning against Dustin Hermanson. Behind in the count, I was just trying to battle up there and put the ball in play. I hit a bloop single to left field, and on touching first base, I thought, "OK, we've got a little life." We kept grinding— Robin Ventura walked, and Jayson Werth had a huge at-bat.

Soon, we were down by only a run, and I remember sitting in the dugout on the edge of my seat, just like everyone else in the stadium. We scratched out the tying run, and the bases were still loaded as our late-season acquisition, Steve Finley, strode up to the plate. He had a great year and was in the right spot at the right time. The only other guy we could've wanted in that situation was Adrian Beltre, who was by far our MVP. Finley hit the first pitch from the lefty who was brought in to face him, and, as soon as he hit it, we knew the game was over. Nobody really thought about the ball going over the fence for a rare walk-off grand slam. We didn't care at the time; we were on the field celebrating our first division title in a number of years. I felt like a kid again, a kid who was relishing the most exciting win of his life.

When I look back on my career, I view my time with the Dodgers as the prime years of my days as a player. For me, there were a lot of great times and a lot of challenging times. Sometimes you can set the bar really high, which is what happened to me after a couple of big years in Toronto. As a player, there were some points when I struggled and consequently was booed. At first, my feelings were really hurt, because I hadn't experienced that before. Having later

gone to the Mets and seeing how tough New York fans can be on *everybody*, I learned that getting booed by the home crowd is merely a part of playing in a big market. I think if I had experienced New York prior to Los Angeles, I wouldn't have been as sensitive in 2003 and 2004. Regardless of the struggles, my time in Los Angeles was special and the majority of people were great to me—especially off the field. Even today, when I come to Los Angeles, I'll see fans, and they thank me for my time there. Those years were some of the fondest years of my career.

Nowadays, in the winters, I have a chance to drive to Dodger Stadium and talk to the young players as part of the team's rookie-development program. When I walk into the ballpark, it evokes my desire to play. There's nothing like walking into an empty Dodger Stadium. Although it's quiet and idle, I can relive all the memories from my days of wearing the white and blue—I can hear the crowd that isn't there, and I can see the action unfolding on the empty field. I love the fact Dodger Stadium is 50 years old. It has plenty of mileage on it, but for me, that's a positive trait. It still looks beautiful and well kept.

This stadium has seen it all: some of the biggest World Series games ever have taken place there, and on the other hand, it has also seen tragic moments. It's almost got a life of its own after 50 years. Many people associate different moments in their lives with things that happened while they were sitting in certain seats. Fans who walk into a stadium that has so much history often relive memories and feelings of years past. As a player, I spoke to many fans who shared with me their memories of coming to games with their dads to watch Koufax and Wills play. Years later, they brought their kids to games to watch Cey and Garvey in the '70s and

Valenzuela and Hershiser in the '80s. They then brought their grandkids to watch my generation play. All of this took place in one glorious stadium.

As a player, it's kind of the same feeling when you walk into the clubhouse. The decor may change a little bit, yet the memories remain. One of my favorite areas to visit is the batting cage, where my most important work was done. I enjoy seeing young players taking their hacks and doing the same drills I was doing as the coaches stand alongside and share their knowledge with this future generation. When I talk to the players, I try to convey how important it is for each of them to come up with their own way of preparing. I stress how important it is to take pride in the little things—the tiniest details. I emphasize that they need to be appreciative of the incredible opportunity they have in front of them, and that they can show their appreciation by respecting the game and the Dodger organization.

Those are the kinds of messages I try to pass on. I could stand there and merely talk about the mechanics of hitting for a little while, but I feel it's more helpful to emphasize the importance of developing their own routines. I want them to know how players before them who had success in the game prepared to play each day. I can only hope to say something that will turn on lightbulbs in their minds that will lead them to improving both as players and as people. These kids are going to be the ones who provide joy and excitement to the next generation of Dodger fans, so it's important for them to be prepared for the responsibility that comes with it.

Shawn Green *played for the Dodgers from 2000 to 2004 and hit 49 home runs in 2001 to set the Dodgers' single-season home run record.*

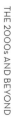

Dodger Organists

Organ music at Dodger home games is a tradition that began in 1942 at Brooklyn's Ebbets Field, when Dodger President Larry MacPhail hired Gladys Goodding, the organist at Madison Square Garden. Goodding added baseball to her sports résumé of hockey, basketball, track and boxing.

During her 16-year tenure with Brooklyn, Goodding often sang the national anthem before games, as she did for other events. She also composed the Brooklyn theme song, titled "Follow the Dodgers." Goodding went to New York in 1936 after attending music schools in St. Louis and Kansas City. Being a part of a baseball team like the Dodgers was of great interest to Goodding, who pitched for a youth team while growing up in Missouri.

When the Dodgers were scheduled to play their final home game in 1957, there was speculation the team was on its way to Los Angeles. Although no official announcement had been made, Goodding proceeded to play songs befitting a funeral procession for the September 24 home finale with the Pittsburgh Pirates. Among her selections that evening were "Am I Blue?" and "What Can I Say, Dear, After I've Said I'm Sorry?"

The Dodgers couldn't have organ music at the cavernous Los Angeles Memorial Coliseum from 1958 to 1961, so fans settled for plastic bugles and other noisemakers. In addition to an organ in the press box for the new Dodger Stadium under construction, the original plans called for a "musical fountain" in center field that would play after every Dodger home run. Those designs eventually were scrapped when the team decided to build pavilions beyond the outfield fence. However, music was still going to be important at Dodger Stadium, and West Germany's Telefunken Company, using the engineers who had designed the acoustical system in Milan's La Scala Opera House, installed the original public address system.

The longest-tenured organists in Los Angeles history are Helen Dell (1972–1987) and Nancy Bea Hefley (1988–present). Dell was already a Dodger fan when Dodger Vice President Red Patterson sent word to an organ company that the Dodgers needed an organist. "I played the national anthem for Red, and that seemed to be a critical point with him," Dell said. "I got about three or four measures into it, and Red said, 'That's the way it's supposed to sound,' which made me feel good."

Hefley began playing the piano at age 4. After high school, she played music in Las Vegas casinos and worked the horse show circuit. Hefley had a chance to spend time with Dell during the Old-Timers' Day luncheons at Dodger Stadium in the early 1990s. They discovered each had played the accordion as a child. And for the 40th anniversary of the stadium in 2002, Hefley shared a "Take Me Out to the Ball Game" duet with Bob Mitchell, the original Dodger Stadium organist from 1962, who still was performing at the local silent movie theater every Sunday at age 89.

PREVIOUS After the 2005 season, the plastic seats were removed and Dodger Stadium returned to its original color scheme from 1962—yellow, light orange, turquoise and sky blue. **OPPOSITE** Tommy Lasorda and Helen Dell in 1981. **OPPOSITE TOP** Bob Mitchell, the original Dodger Stadium organist, visited with Nancy Bea Hefley in 2002. **OPPOSITE BOTTOM** Ebbets Field organist Gladys Goodding.

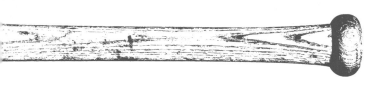

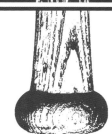

Steve Finley

S teve Finley played in 2,583 regular-season games during his 19-year career, but only 58 with the Dodgers. But the outfielder provided one of the most dramatic moments in franchise history in 2004, when Los Angeles was bidding for its first playoff appearance since 1996.

The Dodgers acquired the 39-year-old Finley on July 31 from the Arizona Diamondbacks in a five-player deal, part of a roster shakeup at the trading deadline. During a two-day period, General Manager Paul DePodesta made deals with the Diamondbacks, the Atlanta Braves, the Boston Red Sox and the Florida Marlins. The Dodgers traded away center fielder Dave Roberts, catcher Paul Lo Duca, outfielder Juan Encarnacion and relief pitchers Guillermo Mota and Tom Martin. Los Angeles acquired Finley, catcher Brent Mayne, first baseman Hee-Seop Choi and pitcher Brad Penny. With a revamped roster, the Dodgers entered August with a 2½-game lead in the National League West.

The NL race came down to the final weekend of the season. Entering the second-to-last day, on October 2, the Dodgers (92-68) held a two-game lead over San Francisco (90-70) in the NL West, but the Wild Card wasn't necessarily a playoff consolation prize, because the NL Central's Houston Astros (90-70) were also in the thick of the race. The Dodgers and the Giants were in the middle of a weekend series in Los Angeles while Houston played host to Colorado. If the Dodgers, having lost the series opener 4–2 on October 1, were swept, there could be three teams at 92-70 and only two playoff spots available.

Things didn't look promising for the Dodgers on October 2 when the team was blanked on four hits through the first eight innings by San Francisco pitchers Brett Tomko, Scott Eyre and Dustin Hermanson.

As the Dodgers trailed 3–0 entering the ninth inning, Shawn Green greeted Hermanson with a leadoff single. Robin Ventura walked, but Alex Cora struck out. Pinch-hitter Jose Hernandez walked to load the bases. Hermanson, pitching for the fifth consecutive day, was gone after Choi's walk forced Green home to make it 3–1. Left-hander Jason Christiansen got Cesar Izturis to hit a grounder, but it was booted by shortstop Cody Ransom, who was inserted into the game in the ninth inning for defensive purposes. Jayson Werth's single off Matt Herges tied the game. The Giants brought in left-hander Wayne Franklin to face Finley, who pulled an 0-1 pitch into the Right Field Pavilion for a walk-off grand slam that gave Los Angeles a 7–3 victory. Finley batted .263 for the Dodgers in 224 at-bats, with 13 home runs and 46 RBI.

The Dodgers set a team record with their 53rd comeback victory of the season, surpassing the previous mark of 52 set by the 1953 Brooklyn Dodgers. Thirteen of the Dodgers' final 14 victories in 2004 were of the comeback variety, and overall they won 26 in their final at-bat. It was the Dodgers' first NL West title since 1995. The Giants were eliminated the following day when Houston clinched the Wild Card.

OPPOSITE Steve Finley watched his division-winning grand slam against the San Francisco Giants in 2004.

Return to the Coliseum

Late in the 2007 season, the Dodgers placed a phone call to Hall of Fame outfielder Duke Snider, inviting him to a special ceremony at the Los Angeles Memorial Coliseum, where the Dodgers played their first four seasons upon moving from Brooklyn. With the 50th anniversary of the Dodgers' arrival in Los Angeles planned for 2008, Snider could imagine a news conference at the team's West Coast version of Plymouth Rock, maybe a few speeches and a photo op in front of the Olympic torches in the front of the facility.

But Snider was startled to hear about a proposed game there. "I'll believe it when I see it," he said with a laugh.

When the Dodgers defeated the Chicago Cubs, 3–2, in 13 innings on September 20, 1961, it marked the final home game in their temporary home. Sandy Koufax pitched all 13 innings, scattering seven hits for his 18th victory of the season. Wally Moon trotted from third base with the winning run after Ron Fairly's two-out single off Chicago's Barney Schultz. After the game, the Dodgers dug out home plate from the ground and the pitchers posed for photos in the outfield, pretending to pull down the left field screen using ropes.

The Coliseum experience, unique to Major League Baseball, produced mixed results for the home team. After a disappointing debut, the Dodgers, in 1959, became the first team in history to win a championship after finishing the previous season in seventh place. In 309 regular-season games from 1958 to 1961, the Dodgers went 172-137 at the Coliseum and averaged nearly 2 million fans per season while finishing seventh, first, fourth and second, respectively.

When the Dodgers pondered another game in 2008, they checked historical photos of the baseball settings because the interior of the Coliseum had since been renovated. The Coliseum field was lowered by 11 feet in 1993, and 14 rows of seats had replaced the running track. This meant less space for another baseball field layout. The original baseball dimension in left field was 251 feet from home plate, with a 42-foot-high screen to compensate for potentially easy home runs. The 2008 measurements, 201 feet and a 60-foot high screen, brought predictions of the scoreboard lighting up like a pinball machine.

On March 29, 2008, the Dodgers and the Boston Red Sox played an exhibition game in front of a record crowd of 115,300. The crowd surpassed the previous mark of the estimated 114,000 fans that witnessed an exhibition between the Australian national baseball team and an American military team during the 1956 Melbourne Olympics. The Red Sox defeated the Dodgers, 7–4. Only four home runs were hit, two by each team. On defense, Dodger manager Joe Torre primarily used a five-man infield, with center fielder Andruw Jones playing behind second base on the skin of the infield and left fielder Andre Ethier covering center, leaving left field unprotected.

ABOVE Roger "The Peanut Man" Owens started working Dodger games during the team's first season at the Los Angeles Memorial Coliseum in 1958.
OPPOSITE Owens was busy during the 2008 exhibition when a record crowd of 115,300 watched the Dodgers and the Boston Red Sox.

In 1994, Chan Ho Park became the first South Korean-born player in Major League history. Park compiled an 84-58 record in nine seasons with the Dodgers. He returned to pitch for the Dodgers in 2008.

China

As a minor league player for 13 seasons, John Lindsey, at age 31, wasn't looking to make history when he reported to the Dodgers' Spring Training facility at Vero Beach, Florida in 2008. His uniform No. 78 indicated Lindsey wasn't expected to make the Los Angeles team, but players like him were always needed during the exhibition season, especially if a split-squad schedule meant the Dodgers were staging games in two cities on the same day.

That was the case in 2008, but Lindsey wasn't asked to take one of the long bus rides along the Florida highway to another team's training facility. Instead, the Mississippi native was chosen to fly to Beijing for a two-game exhibition series against the San Diego Padres as part of Major League Baseball's China Series.

It was a whirlwind trip for the Dodgers under unique circumstances. In the United States, the Dodgers were going to spend Spring Training in both Florida and Arizona. Hall of Famer Tommy Lasorda, at age 80, was left in charge of the Dodgers as manager in Vero Beach while first-year Los Angeles manager Joe Torre brought a group of players that included outfielders Matt Kemp and Andruw Jones and pitchers Chan Ho Park and Hong-Chih Kuo to China.

The Dodgers' traveling party left Florida for China on a Wednesday morning and returned four days later in Arizona, the team's spring home beginning in 2009. In between, the Dodgers played two games in China at Wukesong Stadium, the site of that summer's Olympic baseball competition. The first day in China featured a workout at the ballpark and a visit from Jim Lefebvre, who was the 1965 National League Rookie of the Year when he played for the Dodgers, a former MLB manager and, who at the time, was coaching China's national baseball team. After the workout, the team toured the Great Wall of China.

The first game on Saturday with the Padres ended in a 3–3 tie because MLB officials didn't want the extra innings taxing the pitching staffs. Lindsey hit a single in the second inning, becoming the first Major League player to get a hit in China. The crowd of 12,224 was a mixture of Americans, Chinese government officials and 450 children picked to play baseball by their physical education teachers at 30 schools in the city. After the game, Lindsey walked in full uniform to the metal bleachers and signed autographs. Although Lindsey would spend the regular season with the Triple-A Las Vegas 51s, he will always have that day in 2008 when he made history.

OPPOSITE Former Dodger infielder Jim Lefebvre *(top, third from left)* was the coach of China's national baseball team in 2008 when Los Angeles traveled to Beijing for a two-game exhibition series with the San Diego Padres; Dodger manager of baseball operations Chang-Yen Liao's all-access pass during the 2008 exhibition in China.

ABOVE Top Row: Bill Russell and Maury Wills; *(clockwise from left)* Rick Monday, Rudy Law, Ken Landreaux and Duke Snider. Second Row: Steve Garvey, Eric Karros, Jim Gentile and Wes Parker. Third Row: Ken McMullen, Ransom Jackson, Ron Cey and Dick Gray. Bottom Row: Fred Kipp, Don Newcombe, Carl Erskine and Roger Craig.
OPPOSITE Carl Erskine, Sandy Koufax and Don Newcombe threw out the ceremonial first pitches at Dodger Stadium on Opening Day 2008, which marked the 50th anniversary of the Los Angeles franchise.

2008 and 2009 Playoff Teams

D odger Hall of Fame broadcaster Vin Scully walked to the podium atop a temporary stage set in center field at Dodger Stadium on November 5, 2007 and called the chilly conditions "what the Irish would call a soft day." Scully was there to introduce Joe Torre, who was coming off a successful 12-year run at the helm of the New York Yankees and had attracted a national television audience to the news conference that would present him as the Dodgers' 26th manager in franchise history.

When the regular season began on March 31, 2008 with a 5–0 victory over the San Francisco Giants, all seemed to be looking up. The Dodgers had successfully started the campaign saluting their 50th anniversary since their move to Los Angeles, and with Torre at the helm, there was the feeling that this was a new era of Dodger baseball. That feeling gave way to injuries to such established All-Stars as Nomar Garciaparra, Rafael Furcal, Andruw Jones, Jason Schmidt and Brad Penny. On August 1, the Dodgers were 54-54 when into their clubhouse stepped perennial All-Star Manny Ramirez via a trading-deadline deal. Ramirez combined with up-and-coming young Dodgers Matt Kemp, Andre Ethier and James Loney to ignite the offense.

Still, a late-August eight-game losing streak left the Dodgers at 65-70 on August 29 and facing a pair of Cy Young contenders for the Arizona Diamondbacks in Brandon Webb and Dan Haren, with the season seemingly hanging in the balance. All the Dodgers did was pound the two starters to begin a scintillating 12-1 run to take over first place and eventually clinch the NL West on September 25.

The NLDS against the Cubs brought plenty of excitement, especially in Game 1, when Loney erased a 2–0 deficit with a grand slam in the fifth inning. The Dodgers would not trail again in the series, clinching their first postseason series win in 20 years with a 3–1 victory in Game 3 on October 4. Alas, that was as far as the Dodgers would go, as the Phillies won the 2008 NLCS in five games.

The 2009 season started with a winning trend, as the Dodgers came out victorious in their first 13 home games to set the Major League record for the modern era. Ethier and Kemp established themselves as feared hitters, hitting 31 and 26 home runs, respectively, while each drove in more than 100 runs. The Dodgers held off the late-charging Colorado Rockies to clinch their second straight NL West title in the penultimate game of the season, a 5–0 victory on October 3 at Dodger Stadium. In that game, Clayton Kershaw struck out 10 hitters through five innings to give the Dodgers momentum going into the offseason with an NL-best 95 victories.

In the NLDS, the Dodgers dispatched the Cardinals with a three-game sweep, highlighted by their 3–2 comeback victory in Game 2 of the series, when Los Angeles scored twice in the bottom of the ninth to win. But in the NLCS, the Phillies eliminated the Dodgers again in five games.

OPPOSITE The 2009 NL West champions included *(clockwise from left)* Casey Blake, Manny Ramirez, Rafael Furcal, Matt Kemp, Orlando Hudson, Andre Ethier, James Loney, Russell Martin and manager Joe Torre.

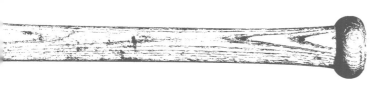

Clayton Kershaw and Matt Kemp

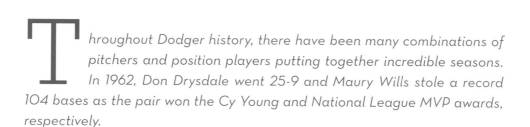

Throughout Dodger history, there have been many combinations of pitchers and position players putting together incredible seasons. In 1962, Don Drysdale went 25-9 and Maury Wills stole a record 104 bases as the pair won the Cy Young and National League MVP awards, respectively.

Only two other times in franchise history had a Dodger pitcher and a position player won those two coveted awards. In 1974, Mike Marshall and Steve Garvey were recognized after leading the Dodgers to the NL pennant. And in 1988, Orel Hershiser's record-setting 59-inning scoreless streak capped off a season in which he paired with Kirk Gibson in willing the Dodgers to the postseason, when they combined heroics on the way to the franchise's sixth World Series title.

In 2011, Clayton Kershaw and Matt Kemp nearly matched their predecessors' collection of postseason hardware, as their respective seasons reached heights rarely seen in Dodger history. Kershaw started the season with a resounding performance before a national television audience, outdueling two-time Cy Young winner Tim Lincecum by throwing seven shutout innings with nine strikeouts in a 2–1 victory over the San Francisco Giants on Opening Day, March 31. That was a sign of things to come, as Kershaw and Lincecum hooked up three more times that season and Kershaw came out victorious on each occasion.

The last of those games was momentous in that the left-handed Kershaw was going for his 20th victory of the season on September 20 at Dodger Stadium. Again, Kershaw was masterful, as he took a shutout into the eighth inning in another 2–1 victory. That night, Kershaw became the first 20-game winner for the Dodgers since 1990. The 23-year-old Texan finished the year at 21-5 with a 2.28 ERA and 248 strikeouts, which gave him the pitcher's Triple Crown, joining Dazzy Vance and Sandy Koufax as the only Dodgers in franchise history to accomplish that rare feat. On November 17, Kershaw was named the National League's Cy Young winner, the 10th such award in franchise history.

Kemp scored the Dodgers' first run of the season in that Opening Day victory, something he did an NL-best 115 times that season. He led the NL with 39 home runs—the first Dodger to do so since Dolph Camilli in 1941—and 126 RBI. He also stole 40 bases, becoming the second Dodger to reach 30-30 status. His .324 batting average was third in the league, and his .586 slugging percentage placed him second. He was the first player to rank in the top three in home runs, RBI, runs, batting average and slugging percentage since Hank Aaron in 1963. On defense, Kemp won his second Rawlings Gold Glove Award in a postseason during which he also garnered the Hank Aaron, Players Choice Player of the Year, Silver Slugger and Stan Musial awards.

THE 2000s AND BEYOND

OPPOSITE Pitcher Clayton Kershaw, *left*, and outfielder Matt Kemp enjoyed All-Star seasons in 2011.

235

Spring Training

Remembering Dodgertown

BY KEN GURNICK

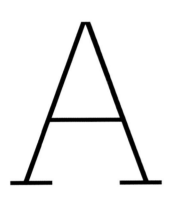

l Campanis would tell stories of when he was field coordinator at Dodgertown, leading 650 ballplayers in calisthenics. It sounded like an exaggeration until he'd produce a yellowish photo.

Dodgertown was the Spring Training brainchild of Campanis' mentor, Hall of Famer and baseball pioneer Branch Rickey, as an extension of another of Rickey's revolutionary ideas, the modern-day baseball farm system.

Dodgertown, the club's spring home from 1948 to 2008, had patriotic roots. The Vero Beach site had been a naval airbase until the military pulled out at the end of World War II. The Dodgers, meanwhile, were tiring of a nomadic training history with stops from southern Florida to Cuba to the Dominican Republic.

Local businessman and airport manager Bud Holman approached Rickey with the idea of turning the base, complete with barracks and airstrip, into a Spring Training camp large enough to handle the Major League roster as well as the Dodgers' 26 minor league teams. Farm team General Manager Buzzie Bavasi visited the base for a site inspection and never got around to checking out other possible sites from Fort Pierce and Stuart, Florida. He found what he was looking for in Vero Beach.

The site provided the essentials for a then state-of-the-art baseball factory: living quarters that slept six to a room, a mess hall, a lounge and plenty of flat land that the team turned into rudimentary ball fields. Nearby apartments were purchased to house staff and media. To keep the players busy off the field, there was Ping-Pong, billiards and a movie theater. Rickey even had a swimming pool installed. The base also included other conveniences,

such as a post office, canteen, barber shop and Western Union office, and the airstrip was so close that when the team plane arrived from Brooklyn—and later, from Los Angeles—players and staff could walk from the tarmac to their barracks. The management, which wanted players to play, not party, deemed the quiet seaside community nearby a boringly good fit.

Not an insignificant consideration to Rickey, the self-contained complex would provide a safe, discrimination-free environment for new Dodger star Jackie Robinson, as well as the many African-American players Rickey envisioned would (and did) follow in Robinson's trailblazing footsteps.

Having all players training at one site also encouraged fraternization, as Vice President Fresco Thompson once wrote, which translated to a familiarity as players moved through the farm system. It also served as a reminder of the franchise legacy, with streets named after Dodger Hall of Famers.

Rickey set up the camp like a college of baseball. He would begin each workout with a lecture, and after calisthenics, players would rotate to various "classes" for baseball basics. Games would follow. At night, staff would meet to discuss the good and bad of the day's events.

Rickey laid out a facility that included the legendary "strings" area for pitchers to work on attacking the strike zone. A set of movable vertical and horizontal strings

PREVIOUS The Dodgers trained in Vero Beach, Florida from 1948 to 2008. **OPPOSITE** Rookie pitcher Karl Spooner pointed to the clubhouse chalkboard in Spring Training 1955.

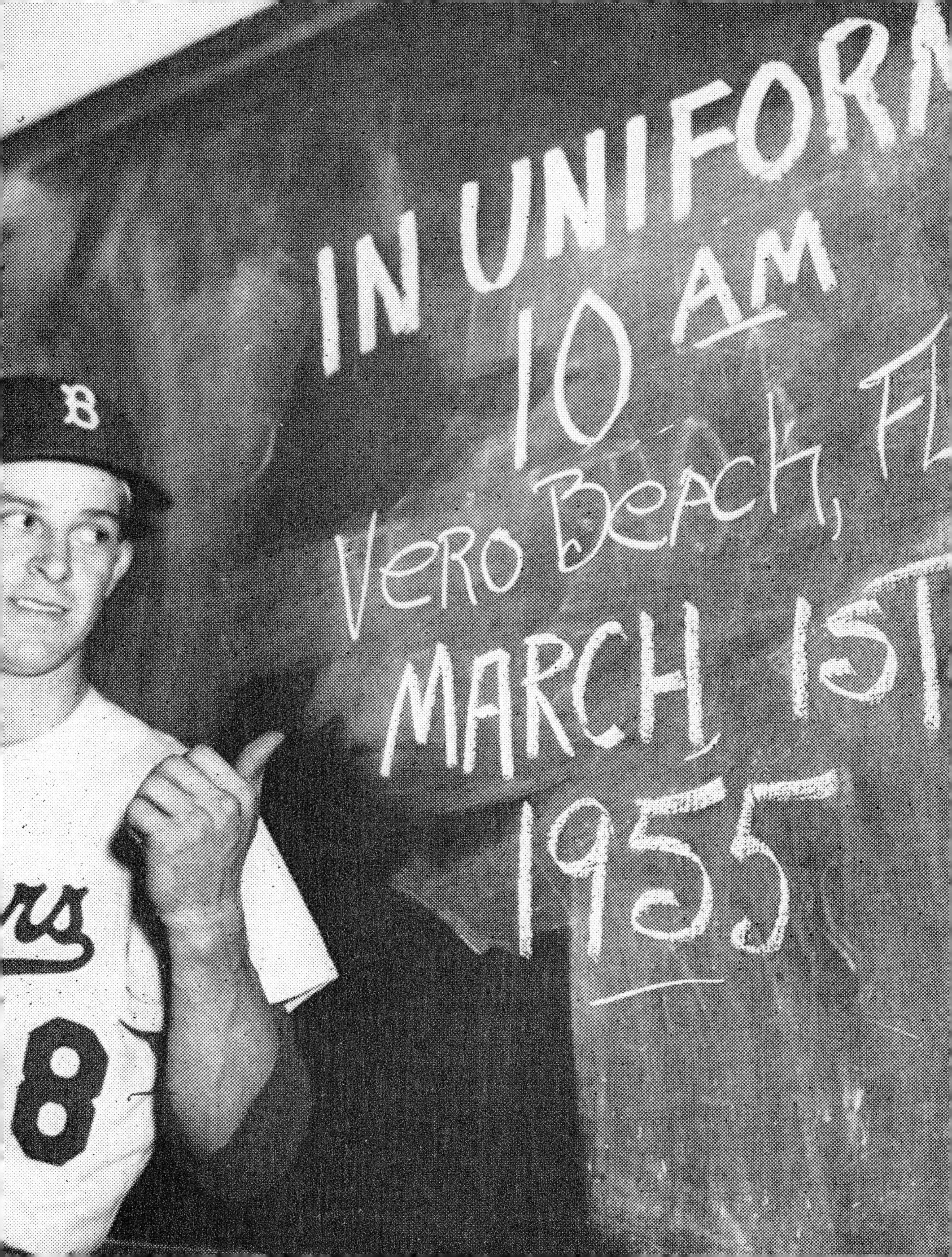
IN UNIFORM
10 AM
VERO BEACH, FL
MARCH 1ST
1955

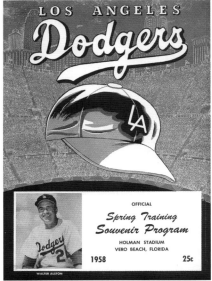

(Clockwise from top left) Brooklyn Dodger players and coaches took a lunch break in 1950; the first "LA" logo appeared on the 1958 Vero Beach program; Tommy Lasorda gave his first spring speech as Dodger manager in 1977; early 1990s brochure for the Dodgers' Campo Las Palmas academy in the Dominican Republic, which opened on March 21, 1987; the academy is located in the town of Guerra, just east of the Dominican Republic's capital city of Santo Domingo; the 75-acre academy is equipped with two full and two half baseball fields, a dining room, kitchen, recreation room and has two two-story dormitories that accommodate up to 100 players; scout Kenny Myers tutored Willie Davis and other prospects in 1961; Dodgertown in Vero Beach named street signs after Hall of Famers, including Vin Scully Way.

attached to poles would form the outline of a strike zone, and the catcher could move the strings to isolate a particular zone of concentration for the pitcher.

Hitters, especially those needing to learn the difference between strikes and balls, would sometimes be sent to the strings area to track pitches and serve as their own umpires, calling balls and strikes before turning toward the catcher to see if they were correct. Rickey installed plenty of batting cages and sliding pits for baserunners. In addition to full fields for games, there were two half fields specifically for infield and baserunning drills.

Campanis would say that Rickey's camp operated with flawless efficiency, and that was no accident. Rickey viewed Dodgertown as a baseball factory that would accelerate the development of young players while bringing "every hidden player potential to the surface."

Dodgertown was the brainchild of Rickey, but it became a monument to his successor, Walter O'Malley, the minority owner who bought out Rickey in 1950 and immediately

upgraded the facility. O'Malley started by turning the mess hall into a dining room, where he and wife, Kay, would stand in the buffet line with players. He gradually upgraded virtually every facet of the place, striving to make it fan-friendly while maintaining its central mission of preparing his players physically and mentally for the upcoming season.

O'Malley, an engineering graduate turned lawyer, envisioned a self-contained retreat, if not an outright baseball resort. To that end, he quickly built a stadium with unobstructed views as a test run for a new 50,000-seat stadium he had planned to replace aging Ebbets Field in Brooklyn. This stadium took 55 days to build, cost $30,000 and was named for Holman. And although it was meant to serve as a dress rehearsal for building a new stadium in Brooklyn, it ended up as a practice run for the development of Dodger Stadium in Los Angeles.

The "stadium" had almost no superstructure and was set against a man-made dirt berm that ringed the field, much as Dodger Stadium would be set against a hillside, with seats

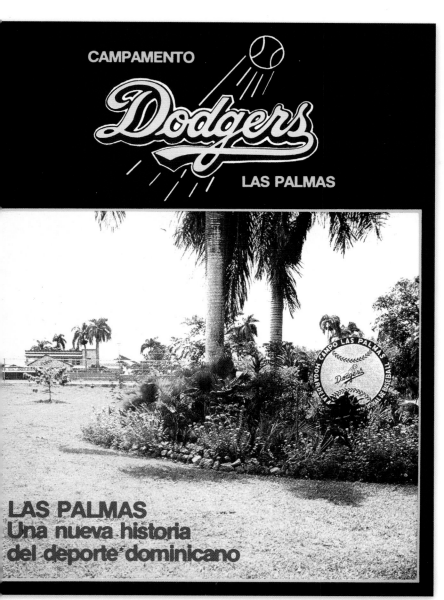

CAMPAMENTO Dodgers LAS PALMAS

LAS PALMAS
Una nueva historia
del deporte dominicano

CAMPO LAS PALMAS
Guerra, D. N.—Republica Dominicana

installed on a cement base. The "dugouts" weren't dug out at all because of the ground water content, so they didn't have roofs, which would have obstructed the view of seat holders. There was no outfield fence originally, only the grass-covered berm where overflow crowds picnicked. On the berm, giant palm trees stood guard and were considered in play. Only after outfielder Dick Allen was knocked out running headfirst into one of those palm trees was a chain-link fence installed in front of the berm.

O'Malley's fingerprints were on everything Dodgertown, from the legendary St. Patrick's Day party (corned beef, cabbage, green beer and green bases) to the late-night poker games in the lounge with the media, to the goodwill visits by foreign teams that illustrated his passion for growing the game internationally, which was continued by his son, Peter, who succeeded him as owner.

Dodgertown, previously idle except in the spring, became a revenue stream when O'Malley turned it into a conference center in 1977, five years after the barracks had

been replaced by hotel-style quarters. Over the years came the additions of tennis and basketball courts and two golf courses. A 23,000-square-foot administration building opened in 1974 with two clubhouses, an infirmary, dining room, lounge and media room. In 1990, a 15,000-square-foot building was added with four indoor batting tunnels. And in 2003, a 30,000-square-foot building rose beyond right field of Holman Stadium with a Major League clubhouse, exercise and training facility and upstairs administration office suites.

A new era began in 2009 when the Dodgers moved Spring Training to Camelback Ranch — Glendale and joined the Cactus League alongside the rest of the western-based Major League teams. But for six decades, Dodgertown stood as a symbol of the team's popularity from coast to coast.

Ken Gurnick *is the Dodger reporter for MLB.com and the co-author of* Rick Monday's Tales from the Dodgers Dugout.

SCOUT REPORT CARD

Name in Full	Erskine,	Carl. (2nd yr)	Pos.	RHP	Age 20
Club	Danville	League	III	Hgt.	5-10 Wgt. 165
Hitting		Power		Bats R	Throws R
Throwing		Power			
Running Speed		Accuracy			
Fielding		Base Running			

PITCHER		
Speed	+	Live F.B.
Curve	A	
Change	A	
Control	A	

APTITUDE

Definite Prospect? **Yes.** Has Chance?

Physical Description (Build, Size, Agility, Etc.) He has good stuff. Lack of expirience   Habits
Bauses him to be a thrower at times instead of a pitcher.
He can stand more weght. He has 4 speeds on the ball and he
Remarks: can major in time. Must be protected in draft this fall

Report By *Cecily Heyh* Date **Aug 3, 1947.**

Note: This card to be used in reporting ALL PLAYERS in Brooklyn organization and any PROSPECTS outside Brooklyn organization.

Early Spring Training

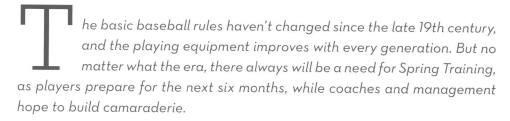

The basic baseball rules haven't changed since the late 19th century, and the playing equipment improves with every generation. But no matter what the era, there always will be a need for Spring Training, as players prepare for the next six months, while coaches and management hope to build camaraderie.

From 1901 to 1948, the Brooklyn Dodgers spent Spring Training at various camps in North Carolina, South Carolina, Arkansas, Georgia, Louisiana, New York, Cuba and the Dominican Republic. Because civilian train travel was restricted during World War II, the Dodgers spent their springs in Bear Mountain, New York from 1943 to 1945. The camp, located an hour's ride from Brooklyn, featured a snow-patched ski jump in the background of the baseball fields. The Dodgers also trained at West Point Academy's indoor field house, which the club was allowed to use during certain hours. The Dodgers leased a military facility in Pensacola, Florida in 1947, one year before the minor leaguers moved into the Vero Beach camp, which served as the team's spring home until 2008.

Major League Baseball teams training in small ballparks eventually realized that exhibition games could become big business, so they began either upgrading or moving to larger sports complexes with enough exercise equipment to rival a five-star health club—a stark contrast to the days when weightlifting was considered taboo. The Vero Beach camp featured the innovative "strings" area, in which a simulated strike zone helped pitchers with their accuracy. But it was more important to supply the players with pinball machines, jukeboxes, Ping-Pong tables and other recreational equipment rather than stock an exercise room with barbells.

"In my day, at the end of the season, you cleaned out your locker and didn't hear from anybody during the winter," said Carl Erskine, who pitched for the Brooklyn and Los Angeles Dodgers from 1948 to 1959. "There really wasn't a year-round conditioning program for the Major League or minor league teams. It was assumed, when you came to Spring Training the following season, that you would be in shape. On the first day, the biggest concern was a player's weight. If you were overweight, they would work on you right away with extra training and drills."

Competition during Spring Training meant players with aches and pains weren't going to complain if they knew there were plenty of prospects ready to take their place. Erskine battled arm problems throughout his career after pitching with an injury during his rookie season.

"During Spring Training, the pitchers did a lot of running and leg drills," Erskine said. "But weightlifting and muscle building was not considered appropriate, especially among the pitchers, because they were supposed to be long and lean.

"I had four pitching coaches, and they were all catchers—Paul Chervinko, Bobby Bragan, Clyde Sukeforth and Joe Becker—because the prevailing theory in baseball was, the catcher knew what the pitcher should do. Now the whole thing has flipped, and the pitching coach, aside from the manager, is the most important person on the staff."

PREVIOUS Dodger greats *(left to right)* Jackie Robinson, Don Newcombe and Roy Campanella all trained at Vero Beach. Newcombe became the first player in baseball history to win the Rookie of the Year, Most Valuable Player and Cy Young awards. With Campanella in 1946, Newcombe played for the first racially integrated baseball team based in the United States in the 20th century. Newcombe started Brooklyn's 1955 championship season by winning 18 of his first 19 decisions en route to a 20-5 record. **OPPOSITE** The 1947 report from Brooklyn Dodger scout Andy High touts minor league pitcher Carl Erskine's "live F.B." (fastball).

(Clockwise from center) Pitcher Johnny Podres and first baseman Gil Hodges rode bikes in a New York gym prior to Spring Training in 1955; Hall of Fame sportswriter Bob Hunter (center, right) was among the media members around a catching prospect; speedster Maury Wills stretched his legs; the 1932 Brooklyn Dodgers trained in Clearwater, Florida; morning drill at Holman Stadium.

Camelback Ranch — Glendale

On November 19, 2007, a special groundbreaking ceremony took place in Arizona to announce an endeavor that was ambitious in both the aggressiveness of its timing and its historic significance: bringing the Los Angeles Dodgers' Spring Training operations to the Cactus League.

That initial plunge into the Sonoran Desert dirt was a joint venture between the Dodgers and the Chicago White Sox. The goal was to build, from scratch over the next 15 months, a state-of-the-art facility to be known as Camelback Ranch — Glendale in partnership with the cities of Phoenix and Glendale.

After six decades of Spring Training being stationed in Dodgertown at Vero Beach, Florida, the Dodgers would be moving closer to their fans. Now, instead of having to make a cross-country flight to see their favorite team in training mode, Dodger fans would be able to drive from Los Angeles in a little more than five hours or take a one-hour hop by plane to Arizona.

"This is the culmination of a long journey designed to give Dodger fans a shorter journey," said Dodger Owner Frank McCourt, who helped spearhead the construction of Camelback Ranch — Glendale. "Our fans are in Los Angeles. Of course, we have fans all over the world, but I'm talking about the critical mass of fans, and they deserve a chance to experience Spring Training."

When the Dodgers opened their first Spring Training in Arizona on February 14, 2009, construction was in its final stages for Camelback Ranch — Glendale's stadium as well as certain areas of the facility. But that day, the 141-acre complex was open for Dodger and White Sox players to begin their preparations for the coming season. The teams spread out their drills among the 12 full baseball fields (not including the main stadium) and three half fields on the grounds. One of the fields matches the exact dimensions of Dodger Stadium, even utilizing the same type of dirt on the warning track as at the Dodgers' Los Angeles home. Also included are 118,000 square feet of clubhouse space for Major League and minor league players.

Dodger fans came to Camelback Ranch — Glendale in droves, several commenting on how, because of its proximity to Los Angeles, they were attending Spring Training for the first time. Even if blue wasn't consistently the most evident shade for those in attendance on the Dodgers' side of the complex, it was easy to tell which side was which: Dividing one half from the other is a curvaceous 1,300-foot-long, 5-acre man-made lake that also serves as an irrigation source for all the greenery on the grounds.

When the final touches were done on the stadium, it was ready to host its first game on March 1, 2009, amid a festive atmosphere for everyone involved. Naturally, the Dodgers and the White Sox were paired in this historic opener, the culmination of the dreams and the hard work of both organizations. The timing of the opening was fortuitous, as the year marked the 50th anniversary since both teams played in the 1959 World Series. The Opening Day celebration gave the 11,280 people in attendance a fireworks show at the end of individual player introductions. *American Idol* winner Jordin Sparks sang an emotion-filled rendition of the national anthem before giving way to ceremonial first-pitch festivities that featured Arizona Governor Jan Brewer, Phoenix Mayor Phil Gordon and Glendale Mayor Elaine Scruggs, who were joined by Dodger manager Joe Torre and White Sox manager Ozzie Guillen.

OPPOSITE Manager Don Mattingly watched spring drills in 2011.

Designed by HKS architects, in Dallas, Texas, Camelback Ranch — Glendale is the largest stadium in the Cactus League, with 10,000 permanent seats and room for more than 3,000 people on the grassy berm beyond the outfield fences. The stadium has shattered many attendance marks and holds four of the top 10 attendance figures in Cactus League history. When the Dodgers and the Mariners played on March 27, 2010, they did so before a Camelback Ranch — Glendale record of 13,583 people.

The architecture features natural stone veneers, tricolor faux staining, rusty metal panels, Gabion wall systems, earth-tone stadium seats and other appointments that blend with the natural desert colors of Arizona. Aside from clear views from every corner of the stadium, fans can also see the Estrella Mountains to the south and the White Tanks to the west. Nearly 5,000 plants and trees are spread throughout the grounds, with an orange grove beyond the left field wall of the Dodger Stadium replica field, which has trees that were transplanted from Dodgertown.

Along with the citrus, a fan-friendly feel was brought to Arizona from the former East Coast Spring Training home in the form of the closeness between the fans and Dodger players. There are no fences or other barriers dividing the players from the fans, just light ropes lining the walkways connecting the fields that allow the Dodgers to stop to chat with people young and old as well as sign autographs and take photos.

Several awards have been presented to Camelback Ranch — Glendale, including the 2010 Facility of Merit Award from *Athletic Business Magazine* and the 2010 Best of the West Award from WESTMARC, a coalition of West Maricopa County, Arizona businesses. In 2009, BallparkDigest.com gave the complex its Editor's Choice Award.

Beyond Spring Training, Camelback Ranch — Glendale is also the year-round home for the Dodgers' player development operations. Once the teams break camp for the beginning of the Major League and minor league seasons, Extended Spring Training takes place at the complex, with minor leaguers working until their assignments to short-season teams start in June. The occasional Major Leaguer might also be found there, rehabilitating an injury.

The Dodger hopefuls enjoy state-of-the-art technology, where coaches utilize video footage of workouts or exhibition games to offer instruction that may help these players reach their big league dreams. The complex also has classroom settings for young international players learning English or others who also look to further their own educational goals.

But what thousands of people have already been able to experience is a rite of spring that brings with it a feeling of renewal that says hope springs eternal, and that the young player practicing bunting in Maury's Pit or throwing a bullpen session may just be the team's next sensation. It all starts at Camelback Ranch — Glendale, and Dodger fans will be able to create memories here for many years to come.

"They thought of everything," said Hall of Famer Tommy Lasorda shortly after the opening of Camelback Ranch — Glendale. "The building is tremendous. The clubhouses are outstanding. The fields are great. It's just a tremendous complex. It's so different in so many ways. We do things according to where we are, and this is good. This is very well done. Fans are going to love it because it's a great ballpark, and it's close to Los Angeles. I think they're going to enjoy coming here."

PREVIOUS Camelback Ranch — Glendale opened in 2009. **OPPOSITE** *(Clockwise from top right)* The Dodgers set a Cactus League attendance record on March 27, 2010. Dodger Owner Frank McCourt sat in front of the stands before the doors first opened for the grand opening of the stadium at Camelback Ranch — Glendale on March 1, 2009. The complex includes more than 118,000 square feet of Major and minor league clubhouse space, 13 full baseball fields and three half-fields.